MW00713731

*Absolutely Every**
BED & BREAKFAST
in
CALIFORNIA
Monterey to San Diego

* almost

TONI KNAPP, EDITOR

Special Contributor:
TRAVIS ILSE

TRAVIS ILSE
PUBLISHERS

POST OFFICE BOX 583
NIWOT, COLORADO 80544

Copyright © 1993 TRAVIS ILSE, PUBLISHERS

All rights reserved. No part of this publication may be reproduced or transmitted in any form or by any means, without permission in writing from the publisher. Requests for permission to make copies of any part of the work should be mailed to: Travis Ilse, Publishers, PO Box 583, Niwot, Colorado 80544.

Cover photograph of California's poppies
by Mark Englert
Courtesy of City of Lancaster, California 93534

Maps by Trudi Peek

Production by Argent Associates, Boulder, Colorado

Printed by Versa Press, East Peoria, Illinois

Library of Congress Cataloging-in-Publications Data

Knapp, Toni
      Absolutely every° bed & breakfast in California (Monterey to San Diego)
   °almost / Toni Knapp., editor. — 1st ed.
         p. cm. — (The Rocky Mountain Series)
      Includes index
      ISBN 1-882092-10-4
      1. Bed and breakfast accommodations—California, Southern—
Guidebooks. 2. California, Southern—Guidebooks. I. Title. II. Series.
TX907.3.C22S685 1993
647.94794'903—dc20

                                                                    93-3094
                                                                    CIP

Printed in the United States of America

A B C D E F 0 5 4 3 2 1

Becky — This one's for us.
Thanks a million.
— TK

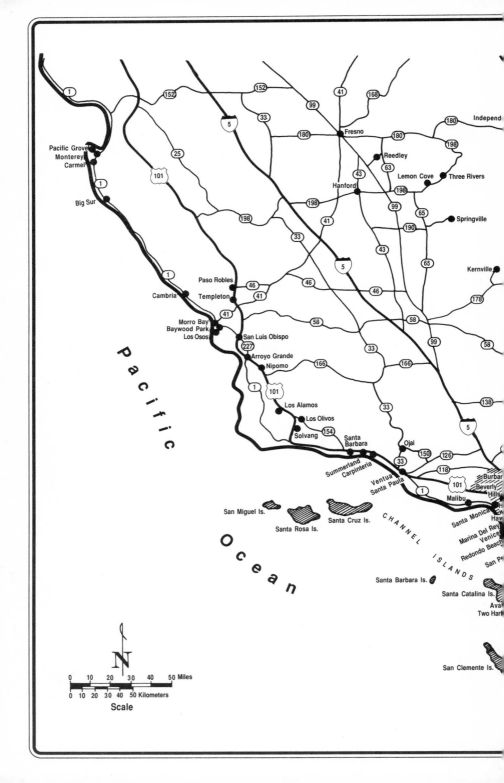

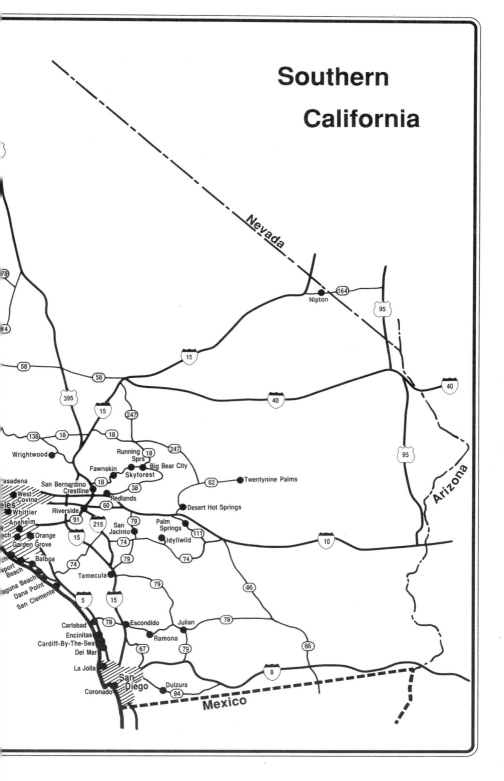

Southern California

CONTENTS

INTRODUCTION

E very time you think you have California pinned down, defined and pigeonholed you turn a corner or hear a conversation, or look up and see something you have never seen or heard before.

This place is a madhouse and magical all at once . . . let's say you are trying to find a parking spot at the local mall on Saturday at about 11 am; you drive around until everyone in the car is dizzy and headed toward grumpy . . . but then you look up through the sunroof in frustration only to see a 747 heading toward China, a flock of migratory birds escaping winter and a huge helium balloon advertising a patio furniture sale.

Madness? Sure. Magical? Of course.

Part of the magic of this place is that you can grab your significant other, pack an overnight bag, hop in the car and in a few hours you can leave the madness behind for a night or a few days at a bed and breakfast that will seem like the other side of the world . . . the quiet, peaceful side . . . in fact, why don't you do that right now?

It's easy, call-up this best friend, this lover, this wife, this husband. Tell her or him to leave work now, while you farm-out the pets or kids or whatever, water the plants and get ready to go this afternoon.

Don't hesitate . . . no excuses . . . life is short . . . do it now!

Now that you've made that date, here are your geographical choices:

CENTRAL COAST. John Steinbeck wrote about it and Portuguese navigator, Juan Cabrillo, was the first to record it on his way south, and Junipero Serra left his missions.

From Monterey and Carmel, scenic Highway One clutches sheer cliffs overlooking a visual feast of lone cypress, crashing surf and incredible seascapes. This is the land of Big Sur Country, a 90-mile stretch of the pristine Ventana Wilderness and Santa Lucia Mountains. Past San Simeon, Hearst Castle and Morro Bay, San

Luis Obispo begins the coastal wine country that extends into Santa Inez Valley. The splendid Central Coast ends between the gentle landscapes of Santa Barbara and Ventura that look out on the Channel Islands.

From here, it's nonstop beach city and surfer chic. And from the beachfront maze of Los Angeles and Orange Counties, it's a straight shot southwest to the refuge of Catalina Island, and southeast to the endless widening beaches that descend into spectacular San Diego.

CENTRAL VALLEY. California's agricultural riches are reflected in Fresno County, the nation's largest agricultural center. More than a million acres of irrigated land produce grapes, figs, cotton and other produce. And—did you know?—more turkeys are raised here than anywhere else in the U.S. But before you pass over the Central Valley, take a moment to be a contrarian . . . if you are avoiding the Central Valley, it's a good bet that most everyone else is too. So if you go to the Central Valley in search of a great B&B experience there is a very good chance that there will be fewer people when you arrive and quite possibly a great B&B that costs less than the more trendy spots.

SIERRA NEVADA. Indians held them sacred, pioneers struggled across them and John Muir worked to preserve them. From the Cascade Mountains, they rise across nearly two-thirds of central California past Kings Canyon at the southern end of the range. Here, Kings Canyon and Sequoia National Park and Sequoia National Forest harbor the world's largest living things: the giant sequoia. Within its borders, General's Highway, Grant's Grove, the Giant Forest and Mineral King are places to wonder at, as are the Wild and Scenic Kern and King Rivers that run through it.

LOS ANGELES. Whither L.A.? It's in Los Angeles County, 4,000 square miles of incomprehensible, unconnected cities and bedroom communities; geographical landscapes that stretch from the Pacific Ocean to the Mojave Desert, and into two vast wilderness areas and mountain ranges. Within these confines lies the Greater Los Angeles Metro Area, a world trade, financial, educational and cultural center, and the most extensive freeway system in the world (never mind that it moves at a snail's pace). At its nucleus is Los

Angeles—yes, indeed—with a thriving and quite spectacular Civic Center, wonderfully preserved historic buildings, and the mini-nations of Chinatown, Little Tokyo, Olvera Street and a few others. Here is a true fantasyland—conspicuous, bizarre, yet oddly middle-America. It's a major gateway to nearly everything, and whatever happens anywhere else, happens here—and usually first.

ORANGE COUNTY. The bastion of conservative politics, citrus groves, 42-mile shoreline and Disneyland stretches south on the Pacific to San Clemente (Richard Nixon's White House) and to the wilderness of the Santa Ana Mountains. Its seventeenth century, Spanish land grant beginnings have evolved into a mind-boggling maze of 31 cities and two million population. Anaheim, once the state's wine capital and quiet citrus-growing area, has blossomed into a mecca of consumate consumerism that revolves around theme parks, conventions and general tourism. But Orange County also offers up San Juan Capistrano, Newport and Laguna Beaches and Dana Point.

THE INLAND EMPIRE, southeast of Orange County, rises from fertile valleys to alpine heights. Here, the surprising Temecula Valley accounts for 97,000 acres of mostly wine-producing vineyards, thirteen significant wineries and a wine festival without equal. Up in the San Bernardino Mountains and National Forest are the alpine jewels of Lake Arrowhead and Big Bear Lake, three ski resorts and the purified air of pine forests.

THE OUTBACK. Awesome deserts overwhelm this vast south-eastern region with otherworldly landscapes. Death Valley National Monument is possibly the most spactacular. It includes within its boundaries the lowest point in the western hemisphere at 282 feet below sea level and is one of the hottest regions in the world (pity the poor mule teams that once hauled 40-ton loads of borax 163 miles out of this valley between 1884-88). Scotty's Castle is here, too, that Spanish-Moorish testimonial to a man with more money than logic. Famous Zambriskie Point (bring your camera) overlooks ancient lake beds that gleam incandescent at sunrise and sunset. The Mojave stretches across southeastern California from Palmdale to north of Los Angeles to the Nevada border. Arrid, desolate and often hostile, it is nonetheless a breathtaking natural wonder.

SAN DIEGO. This is where it all began. Here is the undisputed birthplace of California. Portuguese explorer Juan Rodriguez Cabrillo knew what he was doing when he claimed the area for Spain in 1542. So did Junipero Serra, when he established the first link on his 21-mission chain in 1769. And so has everyone since who flocks to this Pacific Ocean wonderland. Set between mountains and the sea, San Diego County stretches from its 70-mile coast on the west, over the Cleveland National Forest and to the Anza-Borrego Desert State Park and three mountain ranges on the east. That San Diego is also a major U.S. naval, aerospace, educational and research center seems almost incidental.

And there you have it—the best of Southern California, and now it's time to explore this wonderful country through its bed and breakfasts. And almost* all of them can be found in the pages of this guide.

CALIFORNIA BED & BREAKFASTS

The California bed and breakfast industry is as full of surprises—and as big—as the state itself. It's so big, in fact, that in our series of B&B guides (AZ, CO, NM, TX), this will be the only state requiring two volumes. So we arbitrarily divided the state in half at it's middle points, the Monterey Peninsula and Fresno. Now, every B&B in the stunning southern half of California is included for the first time in one comprehensive guide.

Well, almost. The disclaimer (*almost) in our title lets us off the hook for the few that got away, haven't surfaced, or just plain didn't want to be discovered (definitely not in keeping with California character).

The B&B experience is one of the best ways to get an authentic flavor of any state—especially California's southern half, because it's hard to define what it's true flavor is (all cliches stop here). Yes, it's Disneyland, Hollywood and the freeways from Hell. But it's also Big Sur Country, the Channel Islands, the Sierra Nevada and the vast Mojave.

Absolutely Every° Bed & Breakfast in California, Monterey to San Diego (°almost) offers you a choice of more than 247 B&B's in nearly 89 cities and towns in these astonishingly diverse regions: Monterey Peninsula to Santa Barbara, the playgrounds of Orange County, San Diego and Palm Springs, Fresno to the middle of Kings Canyon National Park to the middle of Los Angeles.

It's said there is nothing new under the sun. California is known to be the "first" with the "newest" yet it has its share of the old. Bed and breakfast accommodations in this astonishing state reflect its regions, cultures and history. You can stay in contemporary country inns, simple homestays, cliffside manors, beach cottages, historic Victorians, celebrity enclaves, Zane Grey's pueblo, or the Wrigley Family mansion. And for the truly venturesome there's also the truly odd: a tree house, a sod house, an outdoor woodland shower, a traditional Japanese guesthouse, a clothing-optional hideaway . . . and more.

Every one of the establishments listed in this book—homestays, small and large B&B inns, country inns and small B&B hotels (usually historic)—is a "true" B&B; that is, breakfast is included in the price of the room (a proper breakfast, not lobby fare).

Complete information about each B&B was provided in writing by the innkeepers, and their responses are on file with the publisher.

To ensure the integrity of this guide, *innkeepers did not pay to be listed.*

Our guide is organized in a clear, friendly format that avoids codes, symbols and endless narrative. But we have included little thumbnail sketches of each area listed, to help our readers know where they are headed and what to expect when they get there.

All Reservation Service Organizations (RSOs) and Trade Associations listed in this guide were given the opportunity to list their member B&Bs. Those that responded did so voluntarily, and did not pay to be included.

Some B&B innkeepers (usually homestays) do not want to be contacted directly and list only RSO phone numbers for reservations. Although we believe anonymity is not in the best interest of the traveler, we have included them because, in many instances, they are the only B&Bs in a given area.

The room rates given in this book were current as of press time. This is a volatile industry. Closings and changes in prices and ownership occur regularly. That's why it is advisable to *always* call ahead. Dropping in is chancy and seldom welcomed.

We wish to make clear that the editor, contributing author and Travis Ilse Publishers make no warranty, implied or specific, about the operations or policies of bed and breakfast establishments, RSOs or Trade Associations mentioned in this book. *Absolutely Every* Bed & Breakfast in California, Monterey to San Diego (*Almost)* is not about the bed and breakfast industry. It is intended as a helpful resource for the independent, venturesome bed and breakfast traveler.

One thing is certain. Your bed and breakfast experience in California will surely change the way you travel. We welcome your comments, suggestions and B&B news.

Oh, what a time you are going to have.

ALMOST EVERY*

W e should note here the reason for the "Almost" in our title. First, no one is perfect. Second, we may have missed a B&B for reasons that include our computer going into heat, bad luck, the effects of black holes, springtime at our homebase at the foot of the Rockies, or any of the following reasons:

Innkeepers are busy people who forget to return their survey forms with the information that gets them listed, even after a reminder or two (sometimes three!). Innkeepers are also independent folks who may not want to be listed in any book in general, or our book in particular. Fine, be that way.

Some Reservation Service Organizations (RSOs) don't want their B&Bs listed with information that could allow the traveler to call the B&B directly, thus endangering the RSOs commission. Kind of small-time thinking, but ours is not to wonder why.

Then there is the "Goathead Factor," where someone has been rude or arrogant on the phone, or where we have had consistent complaints from our readers. Here we exercise the right not to list the B&B.

And last, if we missed your favorite B&B, or an innkeeper wants his B&B listed, a gentle note (Travis Ilse, Publishers, PO Box 583, Niwot, CO 80544) will get you in our data base for inclusion in the next edition. And remember that no one on our staff rates, inspects or otherwise judges any of the establishments in this guide. Our job is to provide straightforward information to you, the reader and B&B guest.

BED & BREAKFAST DEFINITIONS

Our guide is essentially a directory of small and medium-sized bed and breakfast inns, hotels and host homes that include a proper breakfast in the price of the room. However, we have exercised our right as travel writers to be inconsistent by including a few "grand" inns with more than 50 rooms (our maximum), because we felt their location and quality warranted inclusion. Though neither absolutely concise nor agreed upon by everyone in the industry, the following definitions may help you determine the differences between types of establishments.

Country Inn: Usually located "in the country"—a rural area far from the maddening crowd. Rooms number between 5-25, and a restaurant on the premises serves other meals.

Guesthouse: A separate unit—cabin, carriage house, etc. Breakfast is either served in the main house or delivered to the guesthouse.

Host Home (or Homestay): The "original B&B." Here, the resident owner rents out from one to three spare bedrooms, typically with shared baths, though private baths are on the increase. With professionalism and competition on the rise, host homes can offer the best of all worlds in terms of rates, service and personal touches.

Hotel: Usually small or historic hotels with between 25-50 rooms, that have been renovated to preserve their historic past and charm.

Inn: The largest and fastest-growing category in the B&B industry—5-15 rooms with mostly private baths, larger staffs and outstanding hospitality.

Lodge: A country inn located in mountain resort and wilderness areas. These are great places for enjoying a wide range of outdoor activities, as well as peace, quiet and solitude.

The Last Word: Whatever you choose, *always* call ahead for reservations—and *always* ask questions: What is the cancellation policy? What exactly is served for breakfast? What are the restrictions, if any? Can breakfast be served in the room? And don't forget to ask for a brochure and a map (some B&Bs are hard to find).

OTHER DEFINITIONS*

(* as they appear in each B&B listings)

With the name of each B&B, we list the mailing address (if any), the actual address, names of resident owners or managers, telephone and FAX numbers. More complete information is provided as follows:

Location: Where the B&B actually *is* relative to the town or area it's in, i.e., directions and miles from the center of town, a highway exit or nearest landmark.

Open: Most B&Bs in California are open all year, but some are seasonal.

Description: On the survey, we ask when a building was built, the architectural style, type of furnishings (antique, rustic, southwestern, primitive) and whether it's on the State or National Historic Register.

Number of Rooms: The number of rooms with private baths, and the number with shared baths (if any).

Rates: Room rates provided by the innkeepers are current as of press time. We have listed the lowest and highest rate that the innkeeper listed prior to publication of this guidebook. Call and ask first, do not depend on the rates listed in this book to be anything more than a point of comparison.

Breakfast: One of the main reasons for staying in a B&B. So we ask innkeepers for accurate descriptions of their morning fare: a full breakfast ranges from the familar eggs, pancakes, meats and fruit to six courses formally served, to a full buffet. Continental is usually fresh coffee, fruit, juices and assorted baked goodies; Continental Plus is somewhere in between: more than Continental and less than full.

Credit Cards: Whether or not credit cards are accepted is listed here. But be prepared—bring a checkbook or travelers checks. Credit cards are expensive for small B&B innkeepers.

Amenities: All the "extras"—hot tubs, swimming pools, afternoon wine and hors d'ouevres, turn-down service, your own llama . . .

Restrictions: Things you can't do or bring: smoking, children, or animals. Some innkeepers have resident pets and would rather not have dog fights everytime a guest rolls up with a BMW load of Rottweilers. Call and ask about restrictions.

Awards: Any awards given to the inn that are recognized and significant to the hospitality industry.

Reviewed: Books in which the B&B has been reviewed—another source of information for the traveler wanting to know more about a particular bed and breakfast.

RSO: Reservation Service Organizations that book B&Bs much as travel agents book hotels.

Rated: Indicates whether a B&B has been rated by the American Automobile Association, American B&B Association, International Inn Society or Mobile Travel Guide.

Member: Membership in professional associations recognized by the hospitality industry.

OTHER B&B GUIDEBOOKS

The following are some good guidebooks where we think the author(s) have really tried to be objective. Before we list them, let us note in passing that if you don't have similar tastes to the guidebook author, you may be in for some surprises.

American Bed & Breakfast Assn. *Inspected, Rated and Approved B&B's & Country Inns.* Midlothian, VA: ABBA.

Annual Directory of American Bed & Breakfast. Nashville: Rutledge Hill Press.

Baillie, Kate. *The Real Guide.* NY: Prentice-Hall.

Barnes, Rik & Nancy. *Complete Guide to American Bed & Breakfast.* Gretna, LA: Pelican Publications.

Bed & Breakfast Guide California. NY: Prentice-Hall.

Bed & Breakfast: Southern California. Los Angeles,CA: Automobile Club of Southern California.

Begoun, Paula. *Best Places to Kiss in Southern California.* Seattle, WA: Beginning Press.

Berkeley Guide to California & Baja: With Trips to Las Vegas & The Grand Canyon. NY: David McKay.

Best Bed & Breakfasts & Country Inns: West. Chicago, IL: Rand McNally.

The Best of the Best in the U.S. Chicago: Chicago Review.

Bree, Loris G. *Affordable Bed & Breakfasts.* Marlor Press.

Brindza, Marie. *Bed & Breakfast Guest Houses & Inns of America.*

Bristow, Linda Kay. *Bed & Breakfast: California: A Select Guide.*

Brown, Karen. *California Country Inns & Itineraries.* Travel Press.

Buzan, Norma S. *Bed & Breakfast North America: A Directory of Small Urban Hotels, Historic Victorian Inns, Country Inns, Guesthouses & Reservation Services.* Bloomfield Hill, MI: Betsy Ross Publications.

Chesler, Bernice. *Bed & Breakfast Coast to Coast.* Malibu,CA: Greene Press.

Dane, Suzanne G. *The National Trust Guide to Historic Bed & Breakfasts, Inns & Small Hotels.* Washington, D.C.: The Preservation Press.

Dane, Suzanne G. & Barbara E. Sturni. *Featherbeds & Flapjacks: A Preservationist's Guide to Historic Bed & Breakfasts, Inns & Small Hotels.* Washington, D.C.: National Trust for Historic Preservation Press.

The Definitive California Bed & Breakfast Vacation & Touring Guide. Travel Press International.

Featherston, Phyllis & Barbara Osther. *Bed & Breakfast Guide for the U.S., Canada, Bermuda, Puerto Rico & U.S. Virgin Islands.* Norwalk, CT: National B&B Assn.

Fodor's Bed & Breakfast Guide. New York: David McKay, Co.

Fodor's Bed & Breakfasts, Country Inns & Other Weekend Pleasures: The West Coast. New York: David McKay, Co.

Fromer's Bed & Breakfast: North America. New York: Prentice Hall.

Gleeson, Bill. *Weekends For Two in Southern California: 50 Romantic Getaways.* San Francisco: Chronicle Books.

Habgood, Dawn & Robert. *On the Road Again with Man's Best Friend: West Coast*. Durbury, MA : Dawbert Press.

Hidden Los Angeles & Southern California. Berkeley, CA: Ulysses Press.

Hitchcock, Anthony and Jean Lindgren. *Country Inns of the West & Southwest*. New York: Burt Franklin Pub.

Killeen, Jacqueline. *Country Inns of the Far West: California*. San Francisco: 101 Productions.

Knight, Diane. *Bed & Breakfast Homes Directory: West Coast*. Watsonville, CA: Knightime Pub.

Lanier, Pamela. *The Complete Guide to Bed & Breakfasts, Inns & Guesthouses*. Santa Fe, NM: John Muir Pubs.

———. *Elegant Small Hotels: A Connoisseur's Guide*. Berkley, CA : Ten Speed Press.

Let's Go: The Budget Guide to California & Hawaii. New York: St. Martin's Press.

Levitin, Jerry. *Bed & Breakfast American Style*. New York: Harper & Row.

———. *Country Inns & Backroads: California*. New York: HarperCollins.

———. *Country Inns & Backroads: North America*. New York: Harper & Row.

Martins, Robyn. *Non-Smoker's Guide to Bed & Breakfasts*. Nashville : Rutledge Hill Press.

McFarlane, Marilyn. *Best Places to Stay in California*. New York: Houghton Mifflin.

Nystrom, Fred & Mardi. *Special Places for the Discerning Traveler*. Issaquah, WA: Nystrom Pub.

The Old-House Lover's Guide to Inns and Bed & Breakfast Guest Houses. Lexington, MA : S. Greene Press.

Olmstead, Gerald W. *The Best of the Sierra Nevada*. New York: Crown.

Peverill, Jan. *Jan Peverill's Inn Places for Bed & Breakfast*. San Clemente, CA: Introductions Unlimited.

Pomada, Elizabeth & Michael Larson. *The Painted Ladies Guide to Victorian California*. New York: Dutton.

Recommended Country Inns: West Coast. Chester, CT: Globe Pequot.

Rundback, Betty and Nancy Kramer. *Bed & Breakfast U.S.A.* New York: Dutton.

Sakach, Timothy & Deborah E. *Official Guide to American Historic B&B Inns & Guesthouses*. Dana Point, CA: American Historic Inns, Inc.

Sealey, Lois. *Bed & Breakfast in the U.S.A. & Canada*. London, England : Home Base Holidays.

Simon, C. & C. M. Solomon. *Frommer's California With Kids*. New York: Prentice Hall.

Soule, Sandra W. *America's Wonderful Little Hotels & Inns*. New York: St. Martin's.

Wageck, Lois. *Motorcycle Bed & Breakfast*. Denver, CO: Arrowstar Pub.

Zimmerman, George. *Travel Writers Recommend America's Best Resorts*. New York : Dutton.

BED & BREAKFAST ASSOCIATIONS

B&B Inns of So. California
Marilyn Watson
2506 Banyan Court
Anaheim, CA 92806

Carmel Innkeepers Assn.
John Nahas
PO Box 1362
Carmelo, CA 93921
(800) 633-2241

Julian B&B Guild
PO Box 1711
Julian, CA 92036
(619) 765-1555

B&B Innkeepers of Southern
    California
Steve Crawford
1400 S. Coast Hwy., Suite 104
Laguna Beach, CA 92651
(714) 676-7047 (800) 424-0053

Hospitality Assn. of Laguna
    Beach
Les Anderson
425 S. Coast Hwy.
Laguna Beach, CA 92651

Beach & Breakfast Innkeepers
    of So. CA
PO Box 15425
Los Angles, CA 90015-0385

California Hotel/Motel Assn.
PO Box 160405
Sacramento, CA 95816
(916) 444-5780

California Lodging Ind. Assn.
2020 Hurley Way, Ste. 390
Sacramento, CA 95825
(916) 925-2915

B&B Guild of San Diego
PO Box 7654
San Diego, CA 92167　?

Professional Assn. of
　Innkeepers Intl.
Pat Hardy & Jo Ann M. Bell
PO Box 90710
Santa Barbara, CA 93190
(805) 865-0707

Santa Barbara B&B
　Innkeepers Guild
PO Box 90734
Santa Barbara, CA 93190-0734
(800) 776-9176

California Assn. of B&B Inns
Sandy Laruffa
2715 Porter St.
Soquel, CA 95073
(408) 462-9191　(800) 284-4667

The following are national B&B associations:

National B&B Assn.
148 E. Rock Rd.
PO Box 332
Norwalk, CT 06851

American B&B Assn.
1407 Huguenot Rd.
Midlothian, VA 23133
(804) 379-2222

Independent Innkeepers' Assn.
PO Box 150
Marshall, MI 49068
(616) 789-0393
(800) 344-5244

Special Places
PO Box 378
Issaquah, WA 98027
(206) 392-0451
Fax: (206) 392-7597

Tourist House Assn. of
　America
RD 2, Box 355A
Greentown, PA 18426
(717) 857-0856

RESERVATION SERVICE ORGANIZATIONS

As the travel agents of the B&B industry, RSOs charge a commission to the B&B on rooms booked. For the traveler, RSOs can be a very convienient source of information about B&Bs, particularly the smaller B&Bs that have little budget for advertising. But calling a RSO is just like calling a B&B . . . ask plenty of questions.

The following list includes California RSOs.

Eye Openers B&B
  Reservations
PO Box 694
Altadena, CA 91003
(818) 797-2055 (213) 684-4428

Small Luxury Hotels
337 S. Robertson Blvd., #202
Beverly Hills, CA 90211
(800) 525-4800

Sleepy Forest Resorts
PO Box 3706
Big Bear Lake, CA 92315
(800) 544-7454

Digs West
8191 Crowley Circle
Buena Park, CA 90621
(714) 729-1669

Bed & Breakfast Homestay
Jack & Ginny Anderson
1605 London Lane
PO Box 326
Cambria, CA 93428

Inns by the Sea
PO Box 101
Carmel, CA 93921
(800) 433-4732

Carolyn's B&B Homes in San
  Diego
416 3rd Ave., # 25
Chula Vista, CA 92010
(619) 422-7009

American Historic Homes
  B&B
PO Box 336
Dana Point, CA 92629
(714) 496-6953

Laguna Beach B&B
33261 Mesa Vista
Dana Point, CA 92629
(714) 496-7050

B&B of Southern California
1943 Sunny Crest Dr.
Fullerton, CA 92632
(714) 738-8361

Rent-A-Room International
11531 Varna St.
Garden Grove, CA 92640
(714) 638-1406

Back Country Tours & Travel
PO Box 1810
Julian, CA 92036
(619) 765-2300 (800) 635-7241

B&B 800
Steve Crawford
1400 S. Coast Hwy., Suite 104
Laguna Beach, CA 92651
(714) 376-0313 (800) 424-0053

California Riviera 800
Steve Crawford
1400 S. Coast Hwy., Suite 104
Laguna Beach, CA 92651
(714) 376-0305 (800) 621-0500

B&B of Los Angeles & Kids
   Welcome
Robin Mahin
3924 E. 14th St.
Long Beach, CA 90804
(310) 498-0552 (800) 383-3513

Resort-II-Me
140 Franklin St., Suite 204
Monterey, CA 93940
(408) 646-9250

Bed & Breakfast International
Harris & Sharene Klein
PO Box 282910
San Francisco, CA 94128-2910
(415) 696-1690
Fax: (415) 696-1699

Megan's Friends B&B
   Reservations
Joyce Segor
1776 Royal Way
San Luis Obispo, CA 93405
(805) 544-4406
Fax: (805) 546-8642

American Historic Inns
Sandy Mimre
31061 Pacific Coast Hwy.
South Laguna, CA 92677
714-499-8070

California Houseguests
International
6051 Lindley Ave. #6
Tarzana, CA 91356

CoHost, America's B&B
Colleen Davis
11715 S. Circle Dr.
PO Box 9302
Whittier, CA 90608
310-699-8427

Four national RSOs worth mentioning will help you find an appropriate RSO elsewhere.

B&B Reservation Services
   World Wide, Inc.
PO Box 39000
Washington, DC 20016
(800) 842-1486

B&B: The National Network
PO Box 4616
Springfield, MA 01101

Innres
7203 Arlington Ave.
Riverside, CA 72503
(800) 777-1460

Treadway Reservations Service
180 Summit Ave.
Montvale, NJ 07645
(800) 873-2392

DEAR TRAVELER:

As you visit B&Bs you leave with opinions, particularly from the great B&Bs where the room was perfect, the innkeeper wonderful, and the food beyond description.

We'd like to hear your thoughts on any B&B that you visit. Just photocopy the form on the following page and fold a bunch of them into the book so that they'll be handy when you travel. If you give us permission to use some or all of your comments in the next edition, we'll send you a free copy of the guidebook if we use those comments.

Let us know what you think. Write to us at Travis Ilse, Publishers, PO Box 583 Niwot, Colorado 80544. We love to get letters.

—*TRAVIS ILSE*
—*TONI KNAPP*

B&B GUEST COMMENT CARD

B&B VISITED: _____

LOCATION: _____

DATES VISITED: _____

COMMENTS, KUDOS, QUIBBLES: _____

_____

_____

_____

_____

❑ I/we grant Travis Ilse, Publishers permission to incorporate some or all of our comments in future editions of this book.

❑ I/we prefer not to be quoted, but here are our comments anyway.

NAME_____ DATE _____

ADDRESS (CITY, STATE, ZIP)_____

_____ PHONE _____

Please mail to: Travis Ilse (CAS), PO Box 583, Niwot, CO 80544

B&B GUEST COMMENT CARD

B&B VISITED: _____

LOCATION: _____

DATES VISITED: _____

COMMENTS, KUDOS, QUIBBLES: _____

_____

_____

_____

_____

_____

❑ I/we grant Travis Ilse, Publishers permission to incorporate some or all of our comments in future editions of this book.

❑ I/we prefer not to be quoted, but here are our comments anyway.

NAME_____ DATE _____

ADDRESS (CITY, STATE, ZIP) _____

_____ PHONE _____

Please mail to: Travis Ilse (CAS), PO Box 583, Niwot, CO 80544

B&B GUEST COMMENT CARD

B&B VISITED: _____

LOCATION: _____

DATES VISITED: _____

COMMENTS, KUDOS, QUIBBLES: _____

_____

_____

_____

_____

_____

❑ I/we grant Travis Ilse, Publishers permission to incorporate some or all of our comments in future editions of this book.

❑ I/we prefer not to be quoted, but here are our comments anyway.

NAME_____ DATE _____

ADDRESS (CITY, STATE, ZIP) _____

_____ PHONE _____

Please mail to: Travis Ilse (CAS), PO Box 583, Niwot, CO 80544

B&B GUEST COMMENT CARD

B&B VISITED: _____

LOCATION: _____

DATES VISITED: _____

COMMENTS, KUDOS, QUIBBLES: _____

_____

_____

_____

_____

_____

❑ I/we grant Travis Ilse, Publishers permission to incorporate some or all of our comments in future editions of this book.

❑ I/we prefer not to be quoted, but here are our comments anyway.

NAME_____ DATE _____

ADDRESS (CITY, STATE, ZIP) _____

_____ PHONE _____

Please mail to: Travis Ilse (CAS), PO Box 583, Niwot, CO 80544

B&B GUEST COMMENT CARD

B&B VISITED: _____

LOCATION: _____

DATES VISITED: _____

COMMENTS, KUDOS, QUIBBLES: _____

_____

_____

_____

_____

_____

❑ I/we grant Travis Ilse, Publishers permission to incorporate some or all of our comments in future editions of this book.

❑ I/we prefer not to be quoted, but here are our comments anyway.

NAME_____ DATE _____

ADDRESS (CITY, STATE, ZIP) _____

_____ PHONE _____

Please mail to: Travis Ilse (CAS), PO Box 583, Niwot, CO 80544

ANAHEIM

Disneyland is here. What else? Well, there's Anaheim Stadium, home of the California Angels Baseball Team from April-October and the L.A. Rams from August-December. There are some nice orange groves. But the place to be is definitely the Orange County coast. Southeast of Los Angeles via I-5.

ANAHEIM BED & BREAKFAST

1327 S. Hickory St.   Anaheim, CA 92805   *(714) 533-1884*
Margot E. Palmgren, Resident Owner

LOCATION	1 mi. from Disneyland. I-5 south Ball Road exit, turn left & cross Harbor Blvd. to Palm St., right 2 blocks to Boysen St., left 1 block to Hickory.
OPEN	All Year
DESCRIPTION	1954 Ranch Casual furnishings
NO. OF ROOMS	3 share 2 baths Single or double occupancy only
RATES	$30-40 Reservation/cancellation policy
CREDIT CARDS	No
BREAKFAST	Continental plus, served in breakfast nook or dining room
AMENITIES	Fireplace in den; TV/radio in rooms; complimentary wine coolers & coffee
RESTRICTIONS	No smoking. No pets. Limit of 2 people per room
REVIEWED	*Bed & Breakfast Homes Directory: West Coast* *Complete Guide to Bed & Breakfasts, Inns & Guesthouses*
RSO	Eye Openers B&B Reservations

ANAHEIM COUNTRY INN

856 S. Walnut   Anaheim, CA 92802   (714) 778-0150
Anna Marie Pischel, Manager

LOCATION	Off Hwy. 5 & Ball Rd., west of Harbor and east of Euclid
OPEN	All Year
DESCRIPTION	1910 Princess Anne Victorian Victorian furnishings
NO. OF ROOMS	6 w/private baths 3 w/shared baths
RATES	PB/$55-80 SB/$70-80 Reservation/cancellation policy
CREDIT CARDS	American Express, Discover, MasterCard, Visa
BREAKFAST	Full, served in dining room Special meals available
AMENITIES	Complimentary sweets; meeting facilities
RESTRICTIONS	No smoking. No pets (resident cat named Oliver). Children over 12
REVIEWED	*American Historic Bed & Breakfast Inns & Guesthouses* *Bed & Breakfast in California* *Bed & Breakfast: Southern California* *Complete Guide to Bed & Breakfasts, Inns & Guesthouses* *Fodor's Bed & Breakfasts, Country Inns & Other Weekend Pleasures—* *The West Coast*
RSO	American Historic Homes B&B B&B of Southern California
MEMBER	B&B Innkeepers of Southern California

SOUTHERN COMFORT BED & BREAKFAST

9321 Thistle Rd.   Anaheim, CA 92804   *(714) 533-1426*
Jim & Jo Parcher, Resident Owners

LOCATION	Halfway between Disneyland & Knott's Berry Farm. Exit I-5 at Brookhurst, south 1 mi. to Broadway (4th traffic light), right to Thistle (1st left turn)
OPEN	All Year
DESCRIPTION	1960s California Stucco Country antique furnishings
NO. OF ROOMS	2 w/private baths 1 w/shared bath (Including 1-bedroom suite w/kitchenette & living room)
RATES	PB/$45-55 SB/$35-45 Reservation/cancellation policy 2-night minimum stay
CREDIT CARDS	No
BREAKFAST	Full, served in dining room
AMENITIES	Hot tub; robes, fireplaces, TV/radio & phones in rooms; complimentary coffee & tea; complimentary pick-up service from Disneyland Travelport
RESTRICTIONS	No smoking. Resident outside cat
RSO	B&B International B&B of Los Angeles B&B of Southern California Eye Openers B&B Reservation Service Rent-A-Room International

ARROYO GRANDE

A lush and gorgeous viticultural area producing some of California's best wines. Tour the vineyards and taste the wines, and be there for the annual Harvest Celebration on Veteran's Day Weekend. Don't miss the coastal sand dunes along the stretch between Pismo Beach and Oceano. Lake Lopez is nice for fishing and waterskiing. About 10 miles southeast of San Luis Obispo via Hwy. 101.

ARROYO VILLAGE INN BED & BREAKFAST

407 El Camino Real   Arroyo Grande 93420   *(805) 489-5926*
Mailing address: 818 Vista Brisa San Luis Obispo, CA 93405
John & Gina Glass, Resident Owners

LOCATION	Northbound, Hwy. 101 Brisco Rd. exit, left at stop, left on El Camino Real. Southbound, Hwy. 101 Halcyon exit, left on El Camino Real
OPEN	All Year
DESCRIPTION	1984 2-story Country Victorian Laura Ashley, antique & Country furnishings
NO. OF ROOMS	7 w/private baths
RATES	$85-165 Reservation/cancellation policy
CREDIT CARDS	American Express, Diner's Club, Discover, MasterCard, Visa
BREAKFAST	Full gourmet, served in parlor
AMENITIES	TV/radio, phones, balconies, skylights & sitting areas in rooms; complimentary afternoon refreshments; fireplace in parlor; small meeting facilities
RESTRICTIONS	No smoking. No pets
REVIEWED	*The Annual Directory of American Bed & Breakfast* *Bed & Breakfast in California* *Bed & Breakfast: Southern California*
RATED	AAA 3 Diamonds Mobil 3 Stars

THE GUEST HOUSE

120 Hart Ln.   Arroyo Grande, CA 93420   (805) 481-9304
Mark Miller, Resident Owner

LOCATION	In the Old Town area. Map sent w/reservation confirmation
OPEN	All Year
DESCRIPTION	1865 New England Colonial New England Colonial furnishings
NO. OF ROOMS	2 w/shared bath
RATES	$47.50-65 Reservation/cancellation policy
CREDIT CARDS	No
BREAKFAST	Full, served in sun room or on garden terrace
AMENITIES	Complimentary afternoon refreshments
RESTRICTIONS	None. Resident Siamese cats
REVIEWED	*American Historic Bed & Breakfast Inns & Guesthouses* *Bed & Breakfast Homes Directory* *Bed & Breakfast in California* *Bed & Breakfast: Southern California* *The National Trust Guide to Historic Bed & Breakfasts,* *Inns & Small Hotels*

ROSE VICTORIAN INN

789 Valley Rd.   Arroyo Grande, CA 93420   *(805) 481-5566*
Ross & Diana Cox, Resident Owners

LOCATION	1-1/2 miles west of Hwy. 101 Northbound: From Traffic Way exit turn left at stop sign at Fair Oaks, 1/4 mi. to Valley Rd., left 1/4 mi. Southbound: Take Fair Oaks exit, turn left on Valley Rd. 1/4 mi.
OPEN	All Year (Closed 2 weeks in January)
DESCRIPTION	1885 4-story Victorian with Restaurant Victorian furnishings
NO. OF ROOMS	7 w/private baths 4 w/shared baths (Including 2 cottages)
RATES	PB/$125-175 SB/$105-150 Reservation/cancellation policy 2-night minimum on summer weekends & holidays
CREDIT CARDS	MasterCard, Visa
BREAKFAST	Full, served in dining room 5-course dinner also included in room rate
AMENITIES	Gardens w/rose arbors, koi ponds & gazebo; full upper deck; queen & king beds, fresh flowers in rooms; onyx fireplace & pump organ in parlor; banquet/wedding facilities; handicapped access
RESTRICTIONS	No smoking. No pets (resident Collie & cat). Children over 16
REVIEWED	*American Historic Bed & Breakfast Inns & Guesthouses* *America's Wonderful Little Hotels & Inns* *Bed & Breakfast in California* *Bed & Breakfast: Southern California* *Best Places to Stay in California* *Complete Guide to Bed & Breakfasts, Inns & Guesthouses* *Fodor's Bed & Breakfasts, Country Inns & Other Weekend Pleasures—* *The West* *Inn Places for Bed & Breakfast*
MEMBER	Professional Assn. of Innkeepers International

BALBOA
(NEWPORT BEACH)

On the Balboa Peninsula and the fun zone of the Newport Beach island complex. Island-hop across the bay on the Balboa Ferry, or depart from here to Catalina Island. Indulge in a Balboa Bar (chocolate-covered banana) and absolutely go see the Victorian Balboa Pavilion.

THE BALBOA INN

105 Main St.   Balboa, CA 92661   (714) 675-3412   FAX: (714) 673-4587
Lalith James, General Manager   Christopher Perera, Manager

LOCATION	Hwy. 55 south (Newport Blvd.) onto Balboa Peninsula, right on Palm St., follow signs to pier, hotel on left
OPEN	All Year
DESCRIPTION	1927 Spanish-Mediterranean Antique & French Country furnishings National & State Historic Registers
NO. OF ROOMS	34 w/private baths
RATES	$97-132 Reservation/cancellation policy 2-night minimum during Memorial Day, 4th of July & Veteran's Day weekends
CREDIT CARDS	American Express, MasterCard, Visa
BREAKFAST	Full, served in restaurant Coffee & juice served in lobby Lunch, dinner & sunset wine & cheese available
AMENITIES	Swimming pool, hot tub, robes; fireplaces, cable TV/radio & phone in rooms; complimentary refreshments for special parties & groups; private conference room; handicapped access
RESTRICTIONS	Inquire about pets
REVIEWED	*America's Wonderful Little Hotels & Inns* *Best Places to Kiss in Southern California* *Best Places to Stay in California* *Hidden Coast of California*

BALLARD
(SOLVANG)

This little hamlet in the Santa Ynez Valley features the little red Ballard Schoolhouse, in continuous use since 1883. There's winetasting at the local vineyards. Very handy to Lake Cachuma Recreation Area. From Santa Barbara, about 27 miles northwest via Hwy. 154, or 50 mi. via Hwy. 101.

THE BALLARD INN

2436 Baseline Ave. Ballard, CA 93463   (805) 688-7770 FAX: (805) 688-9560
Larry Stone & Steve Hyslop, Owners   *Kelly Robinson, Manager*

LOCATION	From Baseline/Edison exit, right on Baseline Ave. for 2-1/2 mi.
OPEN	All Year (Closed Christmas Day)
DESCRIPTION	1984 2-story Victorian Eclectic furnishings
NO. OF ROOMS	15 w/private baths
RATES	$155-185 Reservation/cancellation policy 2-night minimum stay on weekends
CREDIT CARDS	American Express, MasterCard, Visa
BREAKFAST	Full, served in dining room
AMENITIES	Four common rooms, fireplaces in 7 rooms; phone in rooms on request; sun porch; complimentary wine & hors d'oeuvres; meeting facilities; limited handicapped access
RESTRICTIONS	No smoking. No pets
REVIEWED	*Bed & Breakfast in California* *Best Places to Kiss in Southern California* *Best Places to Stay in California* *Complete Guide to Bed & Breakfasts, Inns & Guesthouses* *Fodor's Bed & Breakfasts, Country Inns & Other Weekend Pleasures—The West Coast*
MEMBER	Professional Assn. of Innkeepers International
RATED	AAA 3 Diamonds

BAYWOOD PARK
(MORRO BAY)

Nestled on the coast just south of Morro Bay, it was once named Valley of the Bears by Spanish explorers because of the abundance of Grizzlies. Keep a lookout! The town's location is only a 10 mile southwesterly drive to splendid Montana de Oro State Park.

BAYWOOD BED & BREAKFAST INN

1370 2nd St.   Baywood Park, CA 93402   (805) 528-8888
Edie Havard, Manager

LOCATION	From Morro Bay & Hwy. 1, take Los Osos/Baywood Exit south to Santa Ysabel, west to 2nd St.
OPEN	All Year
DESCRIPTION	1990 Contemporary Theme Suites On Morro Bay
NO. OF ROOMS	15 w/private baths
RATES	$80-160 Reservation/cancellation policy
CREDIT CARDS	MasterCard, Visa
BREAKFAST	Continental plus, served in guestrooms Lunch available
AMENITIES	Woodburning fireplaces, TV/radio/phone, refrigerators & microwaves in suites; complimentary evening wine, cheese & hors d'oeuvres; outside entrances; handicapped access
RESTRICTIONS	No smoking. No children
AWARDS	Los Angeles Magazine 52 Romantic Getaways, Best Inn Within 200 Miles of Los Angeles
REVIEWED	*Inspected, Rated & Approved Bed & Breakfasts*
MEMBER	American B&B Assn.
RATED	ABBA 3 Crowns

BEVERLY HILLS

The city of opulence and excess, Rodeo Drive, Beverly Hills High and upscale zip codes is a good place to see how the rich folk live. But its City Hall is an architectural gem and Greystone Park a refreshing spot. Northwest of Los Angeles via I-10 and I-405. Bring money and perspective.

BEVERLY HILLS GUESTHOUSE

(RSO) *Reservations: (415) 696-1690 FAX: (415) 696-1699*
(800) 383-3513 FAX: (310) 498-0552

LOCATION	On Oakhurst off of Wilshire
OPEN	All Year
DESCRIPTION	1950s Mission Stucco Eclectic furnishings
NO. OF ROOMS	Guesthouse w/private bath
RATES	$55 Reservation/cancellation policy 2-night minimum stay
CREDIT CARDS	MasterCard, Visa
BREAKFAST	Continental, served in main house
AMENITIES	TV/radio in room; handicapped access
RESTRICTIONS	No smoking. No pets
RSO	B&B International B&B of Los Angeles

BIG BEAR
(BIG BEAR CITY & BIG BEAR LAKE)

For a handy alpine escape from the cities and deserts of south central California, this is the place. Summer activities center around the 7-mile lake. In winter, there are three ski resort areas to chose from. And in the fall, there is Oktoberfest, nine weekends of Tyrolean music (can you imagine ?), contests, German food and polkas. From San Bernardino, 30 miles east via I-215 and Hwy. 330.

BIG BEAR BED & BREAKFAST

305 E. Mojave Blvd.   PO Box 101   Big Bear City, CA 92314-0101
Norma Garrigus, Resident Owner   (909) 585-6613   FAX: (909) 585-5775

LOCATION	Hwy. 38 to 1st stoplight, left to Mojave, left 2 blocks. House in on the corner
OPEN	All Year
DESCRIPTION	1978 2-story Home Eclectic furnishings
NO. OF ROOMS	2 w/private baths 2 w/shared bath
RATES	PB/$145 SB/$95 Reservation/cancellation policy 2-night minimum
CREDIT CARDS	American Express, Discover, MasterCard, Visa
BREAKFAST	Full candlelight gourmet, served in dining room
AMENITIES	10-person jacuzzi on upper deck; TV/radio & robes in all rooms, VCRs in 2, 1 w/private deck; game room w/big screen TV & surround sound, video tapes, pool table, wet bar, electronic massage table, exercise equipment; barbeque grill & backyard gazebo; complimentary refreshments; small meeting facilities; computer w/modum, laser printer; FAX & copy machines available for small fee
RESTRICTIONS	No children. Resident dogs in owners' quarters
REVIEWED	*Bed & Breakfast: Southern California*

CATHY'S COUNTRY COTTAGES

600 W. Big Bear Blvd. Big Bear Lake, CA 92315   (909) 866-7444
Bob & Kathy Pool, Resident Owners   FAX: (909) 866-1710

LOCATION	Take Hwy. 18 (Big Bear Blvd.) to Blue Water Rd.
OPEN	All Year
DESCRIPTION	1989 Renovated Country Cottages Country & Victorian furnishings
NO. OF ROOMS	6 w/private baths
RATES	Weekends/$99-209 Mid-week/$59-159 Reservation/cancellation policy
CREDIT CARDS	All
BREAKFAST	Continental plus, served in breakfast parlor
AMENITIES	Rooms w/jacuzzis in front of the fireplace & double-headed showers for two, robes, TV/radio & phones; handicapped access
RESTRICTIONS	Smoking in 2 cottages only. No pets. No children
RATED	AAA 3 Diamonds

EAGLE'S NEST BED & BREAKFAST

41675 Big Bear Blvd. PO Box 1003 Big Bear Lake, CA 92315
James Joyce & Jack Draper, Resident Owners   (909) 866-6465

LOCATION	1 mi. east of Big Bear Lake Village (Hwy. 18)
OPEN	All Year
DESCRIPTION	1983 2-story Log Cabin Some antique & western furnishings
NO. OF ROOMS	10 w/private baths
RATES	$75-165 Reservation/cancellation policy
CREDIT CARDS	MasterCard, Visa
BREAKFAST	Continental plus, served in common area
AMENITIES	Fireplace in common area; all rooms have queen beds w/down comforters & individually controlled speaker systems, some have jacuzzi tubs, TV/radios & phones; limited handicapped access
RESTRICTIONS	No smoking. Inquire about pets (Resident critters: 2 horses, 1 goat, 2 ducks, 2 dogs)
RATED	AAA 2 Diamonds Mobil 3 Stars

GOLD MOUNTAIN MANOR
HISTORIC BED & BREAKFAST

1117 Anita   PO Box 2027   Big Bear City, CA 92314   *(909) 585-6997*
John & Conny Ridgway, Owners   *Donna Doran, Manager*

LOCATION	On the North Shore, 2 blocks past Greenway, right on Anita. (Request brochure for specific directions)
OPEN	All Year
DESCRIPTION	1931 3-story Log Mansion Antique furnishings On two acres
NO. OF ROOMS	1 w/private bath, entrance, & sitting room 6 share 2 full baths (2 have private 1/2 baths)
RATES	PB/$180 SB/$75-155 Reservation/cancellation policy 2-night minimum stay on weekends
CREDIT CARDS	MasterCard, Visa
BREAKFAST	Full, served in dining room or on veranda
AMENITIES	All rooms have robes, most have fireplaces, 2 have private entrances, 1 has private jacuzzi & 1 has a ceiling fan; TV/VCR, billiard table & Dutch shuffle board in activity room; Kimball player piano; complimentary refreshments & afternoon hors d'oeuvres; small meeting facilities
RESTRICTIONS	No smoking. Inquire about children. Resident cat
REVIEWED	*American Historic Bed & Breakfast Inns & Guesthouses* *Bed & Breakfast Guest Houses & Inns of America* *Bed & Breakfast in California* *Bed & Breakfast: Southern California* *Best Places to Kiss in Southern California* *California Country Inns & Itineraries* *Complete Guide to Bed & Breakfasts, Inns & Guesthouses* *Country Inns of California* *Inn Places for Bed & Breakfast* *The National Trust Guide to Historic Bed & Breakfasts, Inns & Small Hotels*
MEMBER	B&B Innkeepers of Southern California
RATED	AAA 2 Diamonds

JANET KAY'S BED & BREAKFAST

695 Paine Rd. PO Box 3874 Big Bear Lake, CA 92315   (909) 866-6800
Sharre Schlarmann, Manager   (800) 243-7031 FAX: (909) 866-6530

LOCATION	Hwy. 18 to Paine Rd. Turn left if coming from the west, turn right if coming from the east. B&B is on the left
OPEN	All Year
DESCRIPTION	1990 2-story Colonial Colonial & Victorian furnishings
NO. OF ROOMS	7 w/private baths 2 w/shared bath Theme suites & rooms
RATES	Inquire for current rates Reservation/cancellation policy 2-night minimum stay on weekends
CREDIT CARDS	American Express, Discover, MasterCard, Visa
BREAKFAST	Full, served in breakfast room, dining room or on patio
AMENITIES	Fireplaces, TV & phone in rooms; complimentary afternoon tea; meeting facilities; handicapped access
RESTRICTIONS	No smoking. No pets. No children
REVIEWED	*Bed & Breakfast: Southern California*
RATED	AAA 3 Diamonds

KNICKERBOCKER MANSION

869 Knickerbocker Rd.   PO Box 3661   Big Bear Lake, CA 92315
Phyllis Knight, Resident Owner   Linda Ford, Manager   (909) 866-8221

LOCATION	From Hwy. 30, go up the mountain & turn right at dam. Right at 2nd stop sign, turn right on Knickerbocker
OPEN	All Year
DESCRIPTION	1922 4-story Log Mansion Antique & Country furnishings
NO. OF ROOMS	4 w/private baths 4 share 2 baths (1 has private 1/2 bath) 1 suite w/private bath
RATES	PB/$95-105 SB/$85-95 Suite/$165 Reservation/cancellation policy 2-night minimum on weekends
CREDIT CARDS	MasterCard, Visa
BREAKFAST	Full, served in dining room
AMENITIES	Hot tub; double-sided fireplace in common area; robes, TV/radio in all rooms, some w/private entrances, jacuzzi tub in suite; complimentary beverages & cookies all day, & evening refreshments; meeting/wedding facilities
RESTRICTIONS	No smoking. No pets (resident dog & cat). Inquire about children
REVIEWED	*American Historic Bed & Breakfast Inns & Guesthouses* *Annual Directory of American Bed & Breakfast* *Bed & Breakfast: Southern California* *Best Places to Stay in California* *Complete Guide to Bed & Breakfasts, Inns & Guesthouses* *Inn Places for Bed & Breakfast* *Inspected, Rated & Approved Bed & Breakfasts & Country Inns* *Recommended Country Inns: West Coast*
RSO	B&B 800
MEMBER	B&B Innkeepers of Southern California Professional Assn. of Innkeepers International
RATED	AAA 2 Diamonds

MOONRIDGE MANOR

43803 Yosemite   PO Box 6599   Big Bear Lake, CA 92315   (909) 585-0457
Francois & Mireille Coinon, Managers

LOCATION	From Big Bear Blvd., north on Moonridge, left on Sand Canyon, left on Teton, & right on Yosemite
OPEN	All Year
DESCRIPTION	1984 3-story New England Colonial Manor French country furnishings
NO. OF ROOMS	1 w/private bath 4 share 2 baths
RATES	PB/$185 SB/$85-145 Reservation/cancellation policy 2-night minimum stay on weekends
CREDIT CARDS	American Express, Discover, MasterCard, Visa
BREAKFAST	Full, served in dining room Dinner & special meals, prepared by French chef, available on request
AMENITIES	Greenhouse w/jacuzzi & mountain views; living room/library w/fireplace & 10 ft. ceiling; master suite w/king bed, fireplace, private balcony, & whirlpool tub for 2; complimentary refreshments
RESTRICTIONS	No smoking. No pets
REVIEWED	*Bed & Breakfast: Southern California*

WAINWRIGHT INN BED & BREAKFAST

43113 Moonridge Rd.   PO Box 130406   Big Bear Lake, CA 92815
Shirin Berton & Jack Culler, Resident Owners   *(909) 585-6914*

LOCATION	From Big Bear Lake Village, take Big Bear Blvd. east 1-1/2 mi. to Moonridge, south (right turn) on Moonridge for 1-1/2 mi.
OPEN	All Year
DESCRIPTION	1981 3-story English Tudor English country furnishings
NO. OF ROOMS	2 w/private baths 2 w/shared bath
RATES	PB/$130-160 SB/$85-110 Reservation/cancellation policy 2-night minimum stay on weekends Inquire about ski & mountain biking packages
CREDIT CARDS	American Express, Carte Blanche, Diner's Club, MasterCard, Visa
BREAKFAST	Full gourmet, served in parlor or solarium Early continental also served during ski season
AMENITIES	Parlor w/TV/VCR, gaming table, complimentary stocked wet bar w/juicer & espresso/cappuccino coffeemaker; robes & radio in all rooms, 1 w/fireplace & jacuzzi tub, 2 w/wet bars; complimentary afternoon wine & hors d'oeuvres
RESTRICTIONS	No smoking. No pets
REVIEWED	*Bed & Breakfast: Southern California* *Weekends For Two in Southern California: 50 Romantic Getaways*
RATED	AAA 2 Diamonds

BIG SUR

Heading north to Big Sur from San Simeon, Hwy. 1 winds precariously for 90 fog-shrouded, sun-dappled miles along high ocean cliffs, past grassy promontories and awesome redwoods and the wilderness of the Santa Lucia Mountains and Ventana (pine) Forest. The town at its center is small and charming, and light-years away from being hippiedom's nirvana. Not to miss: Pfeiffer-Big Sur State Park and the headlands of Garrapata State Park. And yes, the Esalen Institute still offers enlightenment and hot springs. About 35 miles south of Carmel.

POST RANCH INN

PO Box 219   Big Sur, CA 93920   *(408) 667-2200   FAX: (408) 667-2824*
Janice Abell-Donald, Manager   *(800) 527-2200*

LOCATION	On mile marker 45 of Hwy. 1, 28 miles south of Rio Rd. in Carmel
OPEN	All Year
DESCRIPTION	1992 Contemporary Country Inn w/Restaurant Eclectic furnishings
NO. OF ROOMS	30 w/ private baths
RATES	$245-450 Reservation/cancellation policy 2-night minimum on weekends
CREDIT CARDS	American Express, MasterCard, Visa
BREAKFAST	Continental plus, served in Sierra Mar restaurant or room
AMENITIES	Swimming pool, hot tub, robes; fireplaces, CD/cassette players & phone in rooms; complimentary sodas, mineral waters & snacks; small meeting facilities; handicapped access
RESTRICTIONS	No pets
RSO	Small Luxury Hotels

BURBANK

"Beautiful Downtown Burbank" is now one of the largest cities in the San Fernando Valley and a major studio center. Among them, Warner Bros. and NBC offer excellent tours. North of Los Angeles via I-5.

SPIGA'S BED & BREAKFAST

(RSO)	*Reservations: (415) 696-1690 FAX: (415) 696-1699*
LOCATION	North Myers & Magnolia
OPEN	All Year
DESCRIPTION	1940s Mission Ranch and guesthouse Elegant furnishings
NO. OF ROOMS	2 w/private baths 1 w/shared bath
RATES	$60-80 Reservation/cancellation policy 2-night minimum
CREDIT CARDS	MasterCard, Visa
BREAKFAST	Full, served in dining room of main house
AMENITIES	Swimming pool; TV/radio in rooms; handicapped access
RESTRICTIONS	No smoking. No pets (resident cats in main house)
RSO	B&B International

CAMBRIA

Its rugged coastline, pine forests and vantage points for annual whale migrations are prime reasons to visit this jewel of a Victorian English village. Visit the Allied Artist's Association in its 1881 schoolhouse and the coastal Shamel County Park and Leffingwell Landing. Last but hardly least is William Randolph Hearst's Castle, just six miles north of town. About 35 miles north of San Luis Obispo on Hwy. 1.

THE BEACH HOUSE

6360 Moonstone Beach Dr.   Cambria, CA 93428   *(805) 927-3136*
Penny Hitch, Resident Owner

LOCATION	On Moonstone Beach. Exit Hwy. 1 at Windsor, turn west towards the ocean and take the 1st right onto Moonstone Beach Dr.
OPEN	All Year
DESCRIPTION	1970 3-story Clapboard A-Frame Antique & wicker furniture
NO. OF ROOMS	7 w/private baths
RATES	$120-150 Reservation/cancellation policy Inquire about minimum stays during holidays
CREDIT CARDS	MasterCard, Visa
BREAKFAST	Full, served in dining area
AMENITIES	Common room w/large fireplace, fireplaces in some rooms; TV in rooms; complimentary afternoon wine & cheese; telescopes, binoculars, & large ocean-view deck
RESTRICTIONS	No smoking. No pets. Inquire about children
REVIEWED	*Bed & Breakfast in California* *Bed & Breakfast: Southern California* *Best Places to Stay in California* *Country Inns of the Far West: California*
MEMBER	Beach & Breakfast Innkeepers of Southern California

THE BLUE WHALE INN

6736 Moonstone Beach Dr.   Cambria, CA 93428   *(805) 927-4647*
John & Nancy Young, Managers

LOCATION	6 mi. south of Hearst Castle. Exit Hwy. 1 at Moonstone Beach Dr.
OPEN	All Year
DESCRIPTION	1990 Contemporary Cape Cod Country French furnishings
NO. OF ROOMS	6 w/private baths
RATES	$135-165 Reservation/cancellation policy Inquire about minimum stay
CREDIT CARDS	MasterCard, Visa
BREAKFAST	Full, served in dining room
AMENITIES	Fireplaces, TV/radio & phone in rooms; complimentary coffee, tea & afternoon wine & cheese
RESTRICTIONS	No smoking. No pets. Children over 12
REVIEWED	*Bed & Breakfast: Southern California* *Best Places to Kiss in Southern California* *Fodor's Bed & Breakfasts, Country Inns & Other Weekend Pleasures:* * West Coast* *Inn Places for Bed & Breakfast*
MEMBER	American Bed & Breakfast Assn. Professional Assn. of Innkeepers International
RATED	AAA 4 Diamonds

CAMBRIA LANDING INN

6530 Moonstone Beach Dr.	Cambria, CA 93428	(805) 927-1619
Joni Apathy, Manager		(800) 549-6789

LOCATION	On Moonstone Beach. Hwy. 1 to Moonstone Beach Dr. exit
OPEN	All Year
DESCRIPTION	1986 Contemporary Country Antique & country furnishings
NO. OF ROOMS	22 w/private baths
RATES	$75-180 Reservation/cancellation policy
CREDIT CARDS	Discover, MasterCard, Visa
BREAKFAST	Continental, brought to room on tray
AMENITIES	Hot tub; rooms w/fireplaces, TV/VCR, phone & refrigerator stocked w/complimentary wine, champagne or sparkling water; video tapes available at front desk; handicapped access
RESTRICTIONS	No pets
REVIEWED	*Complete Guide to Bed & Breakfasts, Inns & Guesthouses*
RATED	AAA 3 Diamonds

FOG CATCHER INN

6400 Moonstone Beach Dr.	Cambria, CA 93428	(805) 927-1400
Dirk Winter, Owner	(800) 445-6868	FAX: (805) 927-4016

LOCATION	On Moonstone Beach, north of town
OPEN	All Year
DESCRIPTION	1992 2-story English Country Inn Eclectic furnishings
NO. OF ROOMS	60 w/private baths
RATES	$70-150 2-night minimum during summer weekends
CREDIT CARDS	American Express, Diner's Club, MasterCard, Visa
BREAKFAST	Full, served in gathering room
AMENITIES	Swimming pool & hot tub; robes, fireplaces, TV, phones, honor bars, refrigerators, coffee makers & microwaves in rooms; meeting facilities; handicapped access
RESTRICTIONS	No pets
RATED	AAA 3 Diamonds

HOMESTAYS

Reservations: (805) 544-4406   FAX: (805) 546-8642

Four homestays are available in Cambria.

THE J. PATRICK HOUSE

2990 Burton Dr.   Cambria, CA 93428   *(805) 927-3812*
Molly Lynch, Resident Owner

LOCATION	Exit Hwy. 1 at Burton Dr., turn east, house is 1/2 mi. on right
OPEN	All Year
DESCRIPTION	1982 2-story Early American Log House Eclectic furnishings
NO. OF ROOMS	8 w/private baths
RATES	$100-120 Reservation/cancellation policy
CREDIT CARDS	MasterCard, Visa
BREAKFAST	Continental plus, served in dining room
AMENITIES	Fireplaces in most rooms & living room; complimentary appetizers & beverages; handicapped access
RESTRICTIONS	No smoking. No pets
REVIEWED	*America's Wonderful Little Hotels & Inns* *Bed & Breakfast in California* *Bed & Breakfast: Southern California* *California Country Inns & Itineraries* *Fodor's Bed & Breakfasts, Country Inns & Other Weekend Pleasures—* * The West Coast*
MEMBER	Bed & Breakfast Innkeepers of Southern California Professional Assn. of Innkeepers International
RATED	AAA 3 Diamonds Mobil 2 Stars

THE OLALLIEBERRY INN

2476 Main St.   Cambria, CA 93428   (805) 927-3222
Peter & Carol Ann Irsfeld, Resident Owners

LOCATION	Exit Hwy. 1 at East or West Village entrance & follow Main St. to the Inn
OPEN	All Year
DESCRIPTION	1873 2-story Greek Revival Antique & Victorian furnishings
NO. OF ROOMS	6 w/private baths
RATES	$85-115 Reservation/cancellation policy
CREDIT CARDS	MasterCard, Visa
BREAKFAST	Full, served in dining area
AMENITIES	Robes; fireplace in 3 rooms; complimentary evening wine & hors d'oeuvres; small meeting facilities; handicapped access
RESTRICTIONS	No smoking. No pets
MEMBER	Professional Assn. of Innkeepers International
RATED	AAA 2 Diamonds

PICKFORD HOUSE BED & BREAKFAST

2555 MacLeod Way   Cambria, CA 93428   (805) 927-8619
Anna Larsen, Resident Owner

LOCATION	From Hwy. 1 North, right on Main St. for .2 mi., left on Eton, left on Wood, left on MacLeod. From Hwy. 1 South, left on Burton, right on Patterson, left on Wood, right on MacLeod
OPEN	All Year
DESCRIPTION	1988 Contemporary 2-story
NO. OF ROOMS	8 w/private baths
RATES	$85-120 Reservation/cancellation policy
CREDIT CARDS	No
BREAKFAST	Full, served in dining room
AMENITIES	Fireplaces in 3 rooms; TV/radio in rooms; phone in lobby; afternoon complimentary wine & fruit bread turn-of-the-century pub room
RESTRICTIONS	No smoking. No pets. Inquire about children
RATED	AAA 2 Diamonds

PineStone Inn by the Sea

221 Weymouth St.   Cambria, CA 93428   *(805) 927-3494*
Frank & Barbara Banner, Resident Owners

LOCATION	1/2 block from ocean, off Hwy. 1
OPEN	All Year
DESCRIPTION	1990 2-story Contemporary Victorian Country & Victorian furnishings
NO. OF ROOMS	3 w/private baths
RATES	$70-75 Reservation/cancellation policy
CREDIT CARDS	MasterCard, Visa
BREAKFAST	Full, served in lounge or on deck overlooking ocean
AMENITIES	Rooms w/fireplaces, cable TV/radios, private patios or deck; complimentary beverages & afternoon refreshments; kitchen privileges; off-street parking
RESTRICTIONS	No smoking. No pets. No children
REVIEWED	*Bed & Breakfast Homes Directory: West Coast*
RSO	B&B of Los Angeles Eye Openers B&B Reservations

A SUMMER PLACE

PO Box 1516   Cambria, CA 93428   (805) 927-8145
Don & Desiree D'Urbano, Resident Owner

LOCATION	In wooded area overlooking the ocean. Call on arrival for guide
OPEN	All Year
DESCRIPTION	1950s 2-Story Stone Cape Cod Country furnishings
NO. OF ROOMS	2 w/private baths
RATES	$30-55 Reservation/cancellation policy
CREDIT CARDS	No
BREAKFAST	Full, served in formal dining room
AMENITIES	Fireplace, TV/radio & phone in living room; complimentary refreshments
RESTRICTIONS	No smoking. No pets (resident cat & bird). Children 14 & over
REVIEWED	*Bed & Breakfast in California* *Bed & Breakfast Homes Directory: West Coast*

SYLVIA'S RIGDON HALL INN

4036 Burton Dr.   Cambria, CA 93428   (805) 927-5125
Bryane & Sylvia Hume, Resident Owners

LOCATION	Central
OPEN	All Year
DESCRIPTION	1978 California Inn Elegant furnishings
NO. OF ROOMS	8 1-bedroom suites w/private baths, sitting rooms & kitchenettes
RATES	$80-125 Reservation/cancellation policy 2-night minimum on weekends
CREDIT CARDS	Yes
BREAKFAST	Continental, provided in suite
AMENITIES	All suites w/king beds, phones & TV/radio in bedrooms & sitting rooms; hairdryers; microwaves, refrigerators, toasters & coffee makers; complimentary newspaper; handicapped access
RESTRICTIONS	No smoking. No pets. No children

WHISPERING PINES

1605 London Ln.   Po Box 326   Cambria, CA 93428   *(805) 927-4613*
Jack & Ginny Anderson, Resident Owners

LOCATION	In the pines, call for directions
OPEN	All Year
DESCRIPTION	1987 tri-level Contemporary Contemporary furnishings
NO. OF ROOMS	1 suite w/private bath
RATES	$75 Reservation/cancellation policy
CREDIT CARDS	No
BREAKFAST	Full, served in suite dining area
AMENITIES	Hot tub; TV/VCR/stereo w/cassette tapes & phone in rooms; efficiency kitchen
RESTRICTIONS	No smoking. No pets. No children
REVIEWED	*Bed & Breakfast Homes Directory: West Coast*
RSO	Bed & Breakfast Homestay

WHITE WATER INN

6790 Moonstone Beach Dr.   Cambria, CA 93428   *(805) 927-1066*
Ivy Kilgannon, Manager

LOCATION	Close to beach, north of town
OPEN	All Year
DESCRIPTION	1988 Inn Country furnishings
NO. OF ROOMS	17 w/private baths
RATES	Inquire Reservation/cancellation policy 2-night minimum stay on weekends
CREDIT CARDS	American Express, Discover, MasterCard, Visa
BREAKFAST	Continental, served in guest rooms
AMENITIES	All rooms w/robes, fireplaces, TV/radio, phones & refrigerators; 8 have hot tubs; handicapped access
RESTRICTIONS	Smoking limited. No pets
RATED	AAA 3 Diamonds

CARDIFF-BY-THE-SEA

A quiet, peaceful little hillside community of Encinitas. Some of its highlights: the charming beach at Fletcher Cove, and San Elijo Lagoon, a resting place for migratory birds. Lots of trails wind through the area for easy observation.

CARDIFF-BY-THE-SEA BED & BREAKFAST

1487 San Elijo   Cardiff, CA 92007   *(619) 942-2794*
Denise & Michael Foyle, Resident Owners

LOCATION	Across the street from the beach. Exit Hwy. 5 at Santa Fe, right 1/2 mi. to San Elijo, left to house
OPEN	All Year (Closed Thanksgiving & Christmas)
DESCRIPTION	1980 Spanish Mediterranean Southwestern & some antique furniture
NO. OF ROOMS	2-room suite w/2 private baths
RATES	$125 Reservation/cancellation policy
CREDIT CARDS	No
BREAKFAST	Continental plus, served in suite
AMENITIES	King bed, fireplace, wide-screen TV/VCR, stereo, pool table, wet bar & refrigerator in suite; private entrance; complimentary fruit & snack basket & beverages
RESTRICTIONS	No smoking. No pets (resident dog)
REVIEWED	*Bed & Breakfast: Southern California* *Best Places to Kiss in Southern California*
MEMBER	B&B Guild of San Diego

CARDIFF-BY-THE-SEA LODGE

142 Chesterfield   Cardiff, CA 92007　　　　　　　　*(619) 944-6474*
James & Jeanette Statser, Resident Owners　　　　*FAX: (619) 944-6841*

LOCATION	Exit I-5 at Birmingham, west to bottom of hill, left for 3 blocks to first stop sign, then left
OPEN	All Year
DESCRIPTION	1990 Contemporary Cottage Victorian Theme decor
NO. OF ROOMS	17 w/private baths
RATES	$105-250 Reservation/cancellation policy
CREDIT CARDS	American Express, MasterCard, Visa
BREAKFAST	Continental plus, served on patio overlooking ocean
AMENITIES	Rooftop terrace w/gardens, jacuzzi & open-pit fire ring; all rooms w/queen beds, TV/radio & phone, some w/fireplaces & whirlpool tubs; rooftop garden available for private receptions
RESTRICTIONS	No smoking. No pets
AWARDS	1991 Tulip Award for Architecture & Interior Design
REVIEWED	*Bed & Breakfast: Southern California* *Best Places to Kiss in Southern California*
RATED	AAA 3 Diamonds

CARLSBAD
(SAN DIEGO)

This beach resort is a center for commercial flower growing, and is now part of
Oceanside. The town is named after the famous European spa in Karlsbad. The Alt
Karlsbad Haus Museum is interesting.

PELICAN COVE BED & BREAKFAST INN

320 Walnut Ave.   Carlsbad, CA 92008   *(619) 434-5995*
Scott & Betsy Buckwald, Resident Owners

LOCATION	Near the beach. I-5 to Carlsbad Village Dr. (Elm Ave.), west to Carlsbad Blvd., left 4 blocks to Walnut, left on Walnut
OPEN	All Year
DESCRIPTION	1987 2-story Cape Cod Victorian & Southwestern furnishings
NO. OF ROOMS	8 w/private baths
RATES	$85-150 Reservation/cancellation policy Inquire about special rates
CREDIT CARDS	American Express, MasterCard, Visa
BREAKFAST	Continental plus, served in parlor, backyard gazebo, decks, or guest rooms
AMENITIES	Hot tub; 3 decks; fireplaces, TV/radio in rooms; phones in rooms on request; Jacuzzi tubs & Scandia feather beds in some rooms; beach chairs, towels & picnic baskets availalbe; conference room; handicapped access; courtesy transportation from Amtrack, Oceanside & Palomar airport
RESTRICTIONS	No smoking. No pets (resident West Highland Terrier). Children over 12
AWARDS	Inn Times 1991 Top 50 Award
REVIEWED	*Bed & Breakfast in California* *Bed & Breakfast: Southern California* *Complete Guide to Bed & Breakfasts, Inns & Guesthouses* *Fodor's Bed & Breakfasts, Country Inns, & Other Weekend Pleasures—* *The West Coast*
RSO	California Riviera 800
MEMBER	B&B Innkeepers of Southern California California Asss. of B&B Inns Professional Assn. of Innkeepers International

CARMEL

(CARMEL-BY-THE-SEA & CARMEL VALLEY)

It's everything it promises: a seaside village with a picture-perfect beach, dreamlike atmosphere, no fast-food restaurants, parking meters or high-rises. The streets have names but no addresses. Within its four-square-block central area are 90 galleries, 150 restaurants, endless shops, and on a good day, maybe Clint Eastwood. Magnificent offerings include Basilica San Carlos Barromeo del Rio Carmelo (or Carmel Mission), the annual Carmel Bach Festival in July, *Weihnachtsmarkt* opens the holiday season, and always there's Point Lobos State Preserve for sea otters, sea lions and brown pelicans.

CANDLE LIGHT INN

PO Box 1900 Carmel, CA 93921	(408) 624-6451 (800) 433-4732
Sheryl Browney, Manager	FAX: (408) 624-2967

LOCATION	On west side of San Carlos between 4th & 5th, 2-1/2 blocks north of Ocean Ave.
OPEN	All Year
DESCRIPTION	1955 Tudor Country/Ralph Lauren furnishings
NO. OF ROOMS	20 w/private baths
RATES	$119-139 Reservation/cancellation policy 2-night minimum on weekends
CREDIT CARDS	All major cards
BREAKFAST	Continental plus, delivered to room in picnic basket
AMENITIES	Swimming pool; all room w/TV/radio & phones, some w/fireplaces & kitchens; complimentary morning newspaper
RESTRICTIONS	Smoking limited. No pets
RSO	Inns by the Sea
MEMBER	Carmel Innkeepers Assn.
RATED	AAA 3 Diamonds Mobil 2 Stars

CARMEL GARDEN COURT INN

PO Box 6226   Carmel Valley, CA 93924   (408) 624-6926
George Costa, Manager

LOCATION	On 4th at Torres, 1 block east of Junipero
OPEN	All Year
DESCRIPTION	1940's Inn Antique country furnishings
NO. OF ROOMS	9 w/private baths
RATES	$85-175 Reservation/cancellation policy 2-night minimum stay on weekends
CREDIT CARDS	American Express, MasterCard, Visa
BREAKFAST	Continental plus, served in dining area
AMENITIES	Fireplaces, TV/VCR & phones in rooms; complimentary sherry hour
RESTRICTIONS	No pets. Inquire about children

CARMEL TRADEWINDS INN

PO Box 3403   Carmel, CA 93921   (408) 624-2776   (800) 624-6665
Susan Catlin, Manager   FAX: (408) 624-0634

LOCATION	West on Ocean Ave., right on Mission St. for 3 blocks, Inn is on right
OPEN	All Year
DESCRIPTION	1959 Contemporary Contemporary furnishings
NO. OF ROOMS	27 w/private baths
RATES	$69-175 Reservation/cancellation policy
CREDIT CARDS	American Express, MasterCard, Visa
BREAKFAST	Continental, served in guestrooms
AMENITIES	Swimming pool; fireplaces, TV/radio, phones & coffeemakers in rooms; complimentary beverages; meeting facilities; handicapped access
RESTRICTIONS	No children. Inquire about pets
MEMBER	Carmel Innkeepers Assn.
RATED	AAA 3 Diamonds Mobil 3 Stars

CARRIAGE HOUSE INN

PO Box 1900   Carmel, CA 93921   (408) 625-2585   (800) 433-4732
Raul Lopez, Manager   FAX: (408) 624-2967

LOCATION	On Junipero between 7th & 8th, 1-1/2 blocks south of Ocean Ave.
OPEN	All Year
DESCRIPTION	1975 Rustic Shingled Inn Country & some antique furnishings
NO. OF ROOMS	13 w/private baths
RATES	$169-225 Reservation/cancellation policy 2-night minimum on weekends
CREDIT CARDS	All major cards
BREAKFAST	Continental plus, delivered to room on tray
AMENITIES	Fireplaces, robes, down comforters, TV/radio & phone in rooms, some w/sunken bath; complimentary morning newspaper; evening wine & hors d'oeuvres
RESTRICTIONS	Smoking limited. No pets
REVIEWED	*American Historic Bed & Breakfast Inns & Guesthouses* *Complete Guide to Bed & Breakfasts, Inns & Guesthouses*
RSO	Inns by the Sea
MEMBER	Carmel Innkeepers Assn.
RATED	AAA 4 Diamonds Mobil 3 Stars

COACHMAN'S INN

PO Box C-1   Carmel, CA 93921   (408) 624-6421   (800) 336-6421
S. Sharon Clow, Manager

LOCATION	On left side of San Carlos just past 7th St.
OPEN	All Year
DESCRIPTION	1947 2-story English Inn English Provincial furnishings
NO. OF ROOMS	30 w/private baths
RATES	Sgl/$75-145 Dbl/$85-145 Reservation/cancellation policy
CREDIT CARDS	American Express, MasterCard, Visa
BREAKFAST	Continental buffet, served in lobby area
AMENITIES	Tv/radio & phone in rooms; complimentary coffee, tea & afternoon sherry; meeting facilities; limited handicapped access; private parking
RESTRICTIONS	None. Resident dog
RATED	AAA 2 Diamonds

COBBLESTONE INN

PO Box 3185   Carmel, CA 93921   (408) 625-5222   FAX: (408) 625-0478
Raymond Farnsworth, Manager

LOCATION	Exit Hwy. 1 at Ocean Ave., left on Junipero between 7th & 8th
OPEN	All Year
DESCRIPTION	English 2-story Slate & Cobblestone Country Inn Country pine furnishings
NO. OF ROOMS	24 w/private baths
RATES	$95-150 Inquire about suites Reservation/cancellation policy
CREDIT CARDS	American Express, MasterCard, Visa
BREAKFAST	Full, served in dining room
AMENITIES	Terry robes; living room & lounge w/large stone fireplace; fireplace, TV & refrigerator in rooms; complimentary soft drinks, afternoon tea & cookies, & wine
RESTRICTIONS	None
RATED	AAA 2 Diamonds Mobil 3 Stars

CYPRESS INN

PO Box Y   Carmel-by-the-Sea, CA 93921   (408) 624-3871   (800) 443-7443
Michelle McConnell, Manager   FAX: (408) 624-8216
Doris Day, Dennis LeVett & Terry Melcher, Owners

LOCATION	1 block south of Ocean Ave. (main street), at corner of Lincoln & 7th
OPEN	All Year
DESCRIPTION	1929 2-story Mediterranean
	Contemporary Victorian furnishings
NO. OF ROOMS	33 w/private baths
RATES	$82-190
	Reservation/cancellation policy
	Inquire about minimum stay on weekends
CREDIT CARDS	American Express, Carte Blanche, MasterCard, Visa
BREAKFAST	Continental, served in library bar, garden courtyard, or guestrooms
AMENITIES	All rooms w/robes, fireplace, TV & phone; complimentary sherry, fresh fruit & newspaper; library-bar; handicapped access
RESTRICTIONS	None. $15 charge for children & pets
REVIEWED	*American Historic Bed & Breakfasts Inns & Guesthouses*
	Bed & Breakfast in California
	Best Places to Stay in California
MEMBER	California Lodging Industry Assn.
	California Hotel/Motel Assn.
RATED	AAA 2 Diamonds
	Mobil Quality Rated

DOLPHIN INN

PO Box 1900   Carmel, CA 93921   (408) 624-5356   (800) 433-4732
Bob & Lorraine Luce, Manager   FAX: (408) 624-2967

LOCATION	On the east side of San Carlos at the northeast corner of 4th, 3 blocks north of Ocean Ave.
OPEN	All Year
DESCRIPTION	1964 California Colonial Contemporary furnishings
NO. OF ROOMS	27 w/private baths
RATES	$99-195 Reservation/cancellation policy 2-night minimum on weekends
CREDIT CARDS	All the major ones
BREAKFAST	Continental plus, delivered to room in picnic basket
AMENITIES	Swimming pool; king beds, TV/radio, phones & fresh flowers in all rooms, fireplaces in some; complimentary morning newspaper
RESTRICTIONS	Smoking limited. No pets
RSO	Inns by the Sea
MEMBER	Carmel Innkeepers Assn.
RATED	AAA 3 Diamonds Mobil 2 Stars

Happy Landing Inn

PO Box 2619   Carmel-by-the-Sea, CA 93921   *(408) 624-7917*
Robert Ballard, Manager

LOCATION	North of Ocean Ave. on Monte Verde St., between 5th & 6th
OPEN	All Year
DESCRIPTION	1925 Hansel & Gretel Antique furnishings
NO. OF ROOMS	2 rooms/w private baths 5 suites w/private baths, living w/fireplace & wet bar Inquire about honeymoon cottage
RATES	Rooms/$90-110 Suites/$145 Reservation/cancellation policy 2-night minimum stay on weekends
CREDIT CARDS	MasterCard, Visa
BREAKFAST	Continental plus, served in guest rooms
AMENITIES	Garden w/ gazebo & pond; fireplaces, TV/radio in rooms; complimentary refreshments; wedding & reception facilities
RESTRICTIONS	None
REVIEWED	*America's Wonderful Little Hotels & Inns* *American Historic B&B Inns & Guesthouses* *Bed & Breakfast in California* *Bed & Breakfast, U.S.A.* *Best Places to Stay in California* *Complete Guide to Bed & Breakfasts, Inns & Guesthouses* *Country Inns & Back Roads: California* *Fodor's Bed & Breakfasts, Country Inns, & Other Weekend Pleasures— The West Coast*
MEMBER	Carmel Innkeepers Assn.

HILLTOP HOUSE

11685 McCarthy Rd.   Carmel Valley, CA 93924   *(408) 659-3060*
Margaret & Richard Mayer, Resident Owners

LOCATION	Overlooking Carmel Valley. Map will be supplied
OPEN	All Year
DESCRIPTION	1965 California Ranch Contemporary furnishings
NO. OF ROOMS	1 w/private bath 1 w/shared bath
RATES	PB/$90 SB/$75 Reservation/cancellation policy
CREDIT CARDS	No
BREAKFAST	Full, served in breakfast room
AMENITIES	Swimming pool, hot tub, robes; fireplace, radio & phone in rooms; complimentary refreshments; handicapped access
RESTRICTIONS	No smoking. No pets (resident cat). No children
REVIEWED	*America's Wonderful Little Hotels & Inns*

HOLIDAY HOUSE

Camino Real at 7th Ave.   PO Box 782   Carmel, CA 93921   *(408) 624-6267*
Dieter & Ruth Back, Resident Owners

LOCATION	Hwy. 1 Ocean Ave. Exit, downhill & left on Camino Real. House is on ocean side
OPEN	All Year
DESCRIPTION	1905 2-story California Craftsman Antique furnishings
NO. OF ROOMS	4 w/private baths 2 w/shared bath
RATES	$75-90 Reservation/cancellation policy 2-night minimum stay on weekends
CREDIT CARDS	MasterCard, Visa
BREAKFAST	Full buffet, served in living room
AMENITIES	Complimentary snack on arrival & afternoon sherry; some rooms w/ocean views
RESTRICTIONS	No smoking. No pets. Children 10 & over

ROBLES DEL RIO LODGE

200 Punta del Monte   Carmel Valley, CA 93924   *(408) 659-3705*
Glen Gurries, Resident Owner   *(800) 833-0843   FAX: (408) 659-5157*

LOCATION	Carmel Valley Rd. 12-1/2 mi. to Village. Right on Esquiline Rd. (1st right past Village) & follow signs to top of hill
OPEN	All Year
DESCRIPTION	1928 Rustic Country Inn with restaurant Country furnishings
NO. OF ROOMS	33 w/private baths
RATES	$80-120 Reservation/cancellation policy
CREDIT CARDS	MasterCard, Visa
BREAKFAST	Continental plus, served in Fireside Room Lunch & dinner available
AMENITIES	Swimming pool, hot tub & sauna; all rooms w/TV/radio, some have fireplaces; meeting facilities; handicapped access
RESTRICTIONS	No pets
REVIEWED	*American Historic Bed & Breakfast Inns & Guesthouses* *America's Wonderful Little Hotels & Inns* *Bed & Breakfast in California* *Best Places to Kiss in Northern California* *Best Places to Stay in California* *Complete Guide to Bed & Breakfasts, Inns & Guesthouses*

SAN ANTONIO HOUSE

PO Box 3683   Carmel-by-the Sea, CA 93921   (408) 624-4334
Sarah & Rick Lee, Managers

LOCATION	West on Ocean Ave., left on San Antonio at 7th Ave., 5th house on left
OPEN	All Year
DESCRIPTION	1921 2-story Early California Beach English country furnishings
NO. OF ROOMS	4 w/private baths
RATES	$110-150 Reservation/cancellation policy 2-night minimum stay on weekends
CREDIT CARDS	MasterCard, Visa
BREAKFAST	Continental plus, served in guestroom
AMENITIES	Fireplace, TV/radio, phone & refrigerator in rooms; complimentary candies, fruit, & morning newspaper
RESTRICTIONS	No smoking. No pets (visiting cat). Children 12 & over.

SANDPIPER INN AT THE BEACH

2408 Bay View Ave.   Carmel, CA 93923   (408) 624-6433
Graeme & Irene Mackenzie, Resident Owners   FAX: (408) 624-5964

LOCATION	Exit Hwy. 1 at Ocean Ave., left on Scenic Rd., south past 3 stop signs, left on Martin Way, 1 block to Bay View Ave.
OPEN	All Year
DESCRIPTION	1929 2-story Traditional European Country Antiques furnishings
NO. OF ROOMS	16 w/private baths
RATES	$90-175 Reservation/cancellation policy 2-night minimum stay on weekends
CREDIT CARDS	MasterCard, Visa
BREAKFAST	Continental plus, served in lounge at fireside
AMENITIES	Fireplaces & radios in rooms; complimentary refreshments
RESTRICTIONS	No smoking. No pets
MEMBER	California Assn. of B&B Inns Independent Innkeepers Assn.

SEA VIEW INN

PO Box 4138   Carmel, CA 93921   *(408) 624-8778*
Marshall & Diane Hydorn, Resident Owners

LOCATION	On Camino Real between 11th & 12th Sts. Exit Hwy. 1 at Camino Real, left 5 blocks
OPEN	All Year
DESCRIPTION	1910 2-story Victorian Some antique & eclectic furnishings
NO. OF ROOMS	6 w/private baths 2 w/shared bath
RATES	PB/$90-115 SB/$80 Reservation/cancellation policy 2-night minimum stay on weekends
CREDIT CARDS	MasterCard, Visa
BREAKFAST	Continental plus, served in living room & dining room areas
AMENITIES	Fireplace in common room; complimentary afternoon tea & coffee, & evening wine; small meeting facilities
RESTRICTIONS	No smoking. No pets. Children over 12
REVIEWED	*American Historic Bed & Breakfast Inns & Guesthouses* *America's Wonderful Little Hotels & Inns* *Bed & Breakfast: California: A Select Guide* *Bed & Breakfast in California* *California Country Inns & Itineraries* *Complete Guide to Bed & Breakfasts, Inns & Guesthouses* *Country Inns, Lodges & Historic Hotels: California, Oregon & Washington* *Country Inns of America: California* *Country Inns of the Far West: California* *Fodor's Bed & Breakfasts, Country Inns & Other Weekend Pleasures— The West Coast*
MEMBER	Carmel Innkeepers Assn.

SPINNING WHEEL INN

PO Box 3373   Carmel, CA 93921   (408) 624-2429   (800) 633-2241
John Nahas, Resident Owner   FAX: (408) 624-3097

LOCATION	On Monte Verde at Ocean Ave.
OPEN	All Year
DESCRIPTION	1955 2-story Country Inn with restaurant Country furnishings
NO. OF ROOMS	7 w/private baths
RATES	$72-125 Reservation/cancellation policy
CREDIT CARDS	American Express, MasterCard, Visa
BREAKFAST	Full, served in restaurant
AMENITIES	Phone in room; complimentary beverages, fresh fruit & morning paper; VCR's & FAX machine available; off-street parking; airport pick-up; meeting facilities.
RESTRICTIONS	No smoking. No pets
MEMBER	Carmel Innkeepers Assn.

THE STONEHOUSE INN

PO Box 2517   Carmel, Ca 93921   *(408) 624-4569*
Barbara J. Cooke, Manager

LOCATION	On 8th Ave., below Monte Verde. Take Ocean Ave. to Monte Verde, left 2 blocks to 8th St., right to middle of block
OPEN	All Year
DESCRIPTION	1906 2-story Craftsman Antique furnishings
NO. OF ROOMS	6 w/3 shared baths
RATES	$90-125 Reservation/cancellation policy 2-night minimum on weekends
CREDIT CARDS	MasterCard, Visa
BREAKFAST	Continental plus, served in breakfast room or garden
AMENITIES	Glass-enclosed front porch; fireplace in living room; skylights in 2 rooms; complimentary wine & cheese, & cookies & port; small meeting facilities
RESTRICTIONS	No smoking. Children over 12
REVIEWED	*American Historic Bed & Breakfast Inns & Guesthouses* *Bed & Breakfast: California: A Select Guide* *Bed & Breakfast in California* *Best Places to Stay in California* *Complete Guide to Bed & Breakfasts, Inns & Guesthouses*
MEMBER	California Assn. of B&B Inns

SUNDIAL LODGE

PO Box J   Carmel-by-the-Sea, CA 93921   (408) 624-8578
Carole Weir, Manager

LOCATION	1/2 block off Ocean Ave., at Monte Verde & 7th
OPEN	All Year
DESCRIPTION	1929 3-story Bohemian French Country, Victorian & wicker furnishings
NO. OF ROOMS	19 w/private baths
RATES	$105-170 Reservation/cancellation policy 2-night minimum stay on weekends
CREDIT CARDS	American Express, MasterCard, Visa
BREAKFAST	Continental, served in lobby
AMENITIES	Courtyard, TV/radio & phone in rooms; kitchen in some rooms; complimentary afternoon sherry, tea & cookies
RESTRICTIONS	Children over 5

SUNSET HOUSE

PO Box 1925   Carmel-by-the-Sea , CA 93921   (408) 624-4884
Camille & Dennis Fike, Resident Owners

LOCATION	Exit Hwy. 1 At Ocean Ave., left on Camino Real, 2nd building on east side
OPEN	All Year
DESCRIPTION	1960 European Antique & country furnishings
NO. OF ROOMS	3 w/private baths
RATES	$110-150 Reservation/cancellation policy
CREDIT CARDS	No
BREAKFAST	Continental plus, served in guest rooms
AMENITIES	Sitting areas w/fireplaces, TV/radio in rooms; complimentary candy & holiday goodies
RESTRICTIONS	No smoking. No pets (resident dog)
REVIEWED	*Complete Guide to Bed & Breakfasts, Inns & Guesthouses*

SVENDSGAARD'S INN

PO Box 1900   Carmel, CA 93921   (408) 624-1511   (800) 433-4732
Ed & Bonnie Zybura, Managers   FAX: (408) 624-2967

LOCATION	On west side of San Carlos at the northwest corner of 4th, 3 blocks north of Ocean Ave.
OPEN	All Year
DESCRIPTION	1955 Ranch Style Inn Country furnishings
NO. OF ROOMS	34 w/private baths
RATES	$99-190 Reservation/cancellation policy 2-night minimum on weekends
CREDIT CARDS	All major cards
BREAKFAST	Continental plus, delivered to room in picnic basket
AMENITIES	Garden swimming pool; all rooms w/TV/radio & phones, some w/fireplaces & kitchens; complimentary morning newspaper
RESTRICTIONS	Smoking limited. No pets
RSO	Inns by the Sea
MEMBER	Carmel Innkeepers Assn.
RATED	AAA 3 Diamonds Mobil 2 Stars

TALLY HO INN

PO Box 3726   Carmel-by-the-Sea, CA 93921   *(408) 624-2232*
Barbara & Erven Torell, Resident Owners   FAX: *(408) 624-2661*

LOCATION	1/2 block off Ocean Ave. at the end of 6th st., west side
OPEN	All Year
DESCRIPTION	1940 2-story Comstock Eclectic furnishings Originally the private home of nationally syndicated cartoonist Jimmy Hatlo, creator of "Little Iodine" and "They'll Do It Every Time"
NO. OF ROOMS	14 w/private baths
RATES	Courtyard (Views) & Verandas/$105-200 Penthouse & 2-room suites/$185-250
CREDIT CARDS	MasterCard, Visa
BREAKFAST	Full buffet, served in dining room
AMENITIES	Fireplaces in 5 rooms; all rooms w/TV/radio, phones, & duvet comforters; complimentary afternoon tea & after-dinner French Brandy
RESTRICTIONS	No smoking. No children
REVIEWED	*America's Wonderful Little Hotels & Inns*

VAGABOND'S HOUSE

PO Box 2747   Carmel, CA 93921   *(408) 624-7738   (800) 262-1262*
Dennis LeVett, Owner   *FAX: (408) 626-1243*
Honey Spence, Resident Innkeeper

LOCATION	At 4th & Dolores. From Ocean Ave., go west on Dolores for 3 blocks to 4th
OPEN	All Year
DESCRIPTION	1940 2-story English Tudor Antique & country furnishings
NO. OF ROOMS	11 w/private baths
RATES	$79-135 Reservation/cancellation policy 2-night minimum on weekends
CREDIT CARDS	American Express, MasterCard, Visa
BREAKFAST	Continental plus, served in guestrooms or courtyard
AMENITIES	Fireplaces, TV/radio, phone & refrigerators in rooms, some w/kitchens; outside entrances; courtyard w/flower gardens & waterfall
RESTRICTIONS	Extra charge for pets (resident cat). Children 12 & over
REVIEWED	*Bed & Breakfast in California* *Best Places to Stay in California* *California Country Inns & Itineraries* *Recommended Country Inns: West Coast*
MEMBER	American B&B Assn. Carmel Innkeepers Assn. Independent Innkeepers Assn.

VALLEY LODGE

PO Box 93   Carmel Valley, CA 93924   *(408) 659-2261*   *(800) 641-4646*
Peter & Sherry Coakley, Resident Owners

LOCATION	11 mi. east of Hwy. 1 on Carmel Valley Rd., corner of Ford Rd.
OPEN	All Year
DESCRIPTION	1956 & 1979 Rustic Country Lodge Board & Bat buildings In lush garden setting Antique reproductions & country furnishings
NO. OF ROOMS	35 w/private baths Garden Patio Rooms w/patio or deck Fireplace Studios w/1 or 2 connecting bedrooms, living room w/fireplace, kitchen, bar, microwave & patio or deck Fireplace Cottages w/1 & 2 bedrooms, living room w/fireplace, kitchen or wet bar w/microwave, patio or deck w/Hibachi
RATES	Garden Patio Rooms/$95-110 Fireplace Studios/$125-265 Fireplace Cottages/$150-260 Reservation/cancellation policy 2-night minimum on weekends .
CREDIT CARDS	American Express, MasterCard, Visa
BREAKFAST	Continental plus, served in dining room or guestrooms
AMENITIES	Heated swimming pool, hot tub, sauna, exercise room; fresh cut flowers, TV/clock radio & phone in rooms; complimentary newspaper w/breakfast; meeting/conference center; 2 rooms w/handicapped access
RESTRICTIONS	Extra charge for pets (resident dog)
REVIEWED	*Annual Directory of American Bed & Breakfasts* *Bed & Breakfast in California* *Complete Guide to Bed & Breakfasts, Inns & Guesthouses*
RATED	AAA 3 Diamonds Mobil 3 Stars

WAYSIDE INN

PO Box 1900   Carmel, CA 93921   *(408) 624-5336   (800) 433-4732*
Raul Lopez, Manager   *FAX: (408) 624-2967*

LOCATION	On the southeast corner of 7th & Mission, 1 block south of Ocean Ave.
OPEN	All Year
DESCRIPTION	1949 Colonial Early American furnishings
NO. OF ROOMS	22 w/private baths
RATES	$99-225 Reservation/cancellation policy 2-night minimum on weekends
CREDIT CARDS	All the major ones
BREAKFAST	Continental plus, delivered to room in picnic basket
AMENITIES	All rooms w/TV/radio & phones, some w/fireplaces & kitchens; complimentary morning newspapers
RESTRICTIONS	Smoking limited
RSO	Inns by the Sea
MEMBER	Carmel Innkeepers Assn.
RATED	AAA 2 Diamonds Mobil 2 Stars

CARPINTERIA

A little resort community about 12 miles southeast of Santa Barbara via Hwy. 101, known for its wide beach and natural reef breakwater. Camping out on the beach can be done in style at 18-acre Carpinteria State Beach. The town blooms as a commercial flower-growing center.

CARPINTERIA BEACH CONDO

4902 Sandyland, #245   Carpinteria, CA 93013   *(805) 684-1579*
Mailing address: D&B Schroeder Ranch 1825 Cravens Ln. Carpinteria
Bev & Don Schroeder, Resident Owners

LOCATION	South Bound: Exit Hwy. 101 at Linden Ave., 9 blocks west to ocean & Sandyland North Bound: Exit Hwy. 101 at Casitas Pass, west to ocean
OPEN	All Year
DESCRIPTION	1978 Frame & Stucco Condo Tropical furnishings
NO. OF ROOMS	1-bedroom condo w/private bath, living room & fully equipped mini-kitchen
RATES	$60-75 Reservation/cancellation policy
CREDIT CARDS	No
BREAKFAST	Continental, provided in kitchen Other meals available if desired
AMENITIES	Swimming pool & hot tub; TV/radio; pick lemons & avacados at hosts' nearby ranch; guest privileges at Polo & Racquet Club for small charge
RESTRICTIONS	No smoking. No pets
REVIEWED	*The Annual Directory of American Bed & Breakfast* *Bed & Breakfast North America* *Bed & Breakfast U.S.A.* *The Non-Smokers Guide to Bed & Breakfasts*

CORONADO

Cross over the arching Coronado Bridge, or take the leisurely route via vintage ferry to this dream of a place on the Silver Strand Peninsula in San Diego Bay. Stately Victorians mix it up with custom homes and classy condos. And at the north end of the strand, the U.S. Naval Air Station provides the excitement of high-tech air- and seacraft. Good reasons to here: Silver Strand State Beach; the Coronado Municipal Golf Course bordering the Bay; the public Tennis Center and High Tea at the historic Hotel del Coronado.

CORONADO VILLAGE INN

1017 Park Place   Coronado, CA 92118   *(619) 435-9318*
Brent & Elizabeth Bogh, Resident Owners
Tony & Jeanne DiFulvio, Resident Managers

LOCATION	1/2 block south of 10th & Orange, off of I-5 exit at Rte. 75 Coronado Bridge
OPEN	All Year
DESCRIPTION	1929 3-story Mediterranean European furnishings Coronado Historic Register
NO. OF ROOMS	14 w/private baths
RATES	$50-90 Reservation/cancellation policy
CREDIT CARDS	American Express, MasterCard, Visa
BREAKFAST	Continental, served in guest kitchen
AMENITIES	TV/radio & phones in rooms
RESTRICTIONS	No pets (resident cat)
REVIEWED	*Bed & Breakfast U.S.A.* *Best Places to Stay in California* *Complete Guide to Bed & Breakfasts, Inns & Guesthouses*
MEMBER	National Bed & Breakfast Assn. Tourist House Assn.

CRESTLINE

An alpine gem in the San Bernardino Mountains is the smallest of a chain of resorts along breath-catching "Rim of the World Drive." Great fishing and boating facilities can be found at Lake Gregory Regional Park, and Silverwood Lakes State Recreation Area. North of San Bernardino via I-215 and scenic Rt. 18.

CEDAR & PINE BED & BREAKFAST

PO Box 1173   Crestline, CA 92325   *(909) 338-5866*
B. A. Storm, Resident Owner

LOCATION	In wooded area. Map is sent on receipt of deposit
OPEN	All Year
DESCRIPTION	1981 2-story Cedar & Pine French Country furnishings
NO. OF ROOMS	1 w/private bath 2 w/shared bath
RATES	PB/$60-80 SB/$45-60 Senior Discounts Reservation/cancellation policy
CREDIT CARDS	No
BREAKFAST	Continental plus; served in dining room, guestroom, or on deck Box lunches available w/advance notice
AMENITIES	Large deck, complimentary late afternoon refreshments; fireplace in living room; game room w/TV/VCR & videos, pool table, computer games, chess & puzzles, books & magazines; meeting facilities
RESTRICTIONS	No smoking. Resident cat. No children. 10:30 p.m. curfew

CUCAMONGA
(RANCHO)

The site of California's first "wine country," Rancho Cucamonga, or just "Cucamonga" to the locals, is 37 miles east of Los Angeles in the foothills of the San Gabriel Mountains.

CHRISTMAS HOUSE
BED & BREAKFAST INN

9240 Archibald Ave.   Rancho Cucamonga, CA 91730   · (909) 980-6450
Janice Ilsley, Owner   *Sandra Dirks, Resident Manager*

LOCATION	1-1/4 mi. north of I-10 on Archibald Ave. exit
OPEN	All Year
DESCRIPTION	1904 2-story Queen Anne Victorian with wraparound verandah Victorian furnishings City of Rancho Cucamonga Historic Landmark
NO. OF ROOMS	4 w/private baths 2 w/shared bath
RATES	PB/$115-145 SB/$60-70 Reservation/cancellation policy Weekday corporate rates
CREDIT CARDS	American Express, Discover, MasterCard, Visa
BREAKFAST	Full, served in dining room or some guestrooms
AMENITIES	All rooms have robes, 2 have private hot tubs, 3 have fireplaces, 1 has TV/VCR, movies & phone; TV/radios available for other rooms; complimentary coffee & tea; meeting/wedding facilities; inquire about Murder Mysteries nights
RESTRICTIONS	No smoking
AWARDS	Rancho Cucamonga 1987 Award of Design Excellence
REVIEWED	*American Historic Bed & Breakfast Inns & Guesthouses* *Bed & Breakfast in California* *Bed & Breakfast: Southern California* *Complete Guide to Bed & Breakfasts, Inns & Guesthouses* *Fodor's Bed & Breakfasts, Country Inns & Other Weekend Pleasures— The West Coast*
MEMBER	Bed & Breakfast Innkeepers of Southern California

DANA POINT

This seaport and major whale-watching spot has changed since it was immortalized in Richard Henry Dana's *Two Years Before the Mast*. A 2,500-boat marina now fills the famous secluded harbor, along with multitudes of shops and restaurants. Not to be missed: the Orange County Marine Institute's floating laboratory; the full-sized replica of Dana's ship, *The Pilgrim* and the Dana Point Light House. The annual Harbor Whale Festival in Feb.-Mar. is a very big event. On the Orange County Coast, 10 miles south of Laguna Beach via I-5 and Hwy. 1.

BLUE LANTERN INN

34343 Street of the Blue Lantern   Dana Point, CA 92629
Tom Taylor, Manager   *(714) 661-1304   FAX: (714) 496-1483*

LOCATION	On the bluff overlooking Dana Point Yacht Harbor
OPEN	All Year
DESCRIPTION	1990 Cape Cod Country furnishings
NO. OF ROOMS	29 w/shared bath
RATES	$135-200 Reservation/cancellation policy
CREDIT CARDS	American Express, MasterCard, Visa
BREAKFAST	Full gourmet, served in dining area, guest rooms, or on private decks
AMENITIES	Jacuzzi tubs & robes; most rooms w/private sundecks; fireplaces, TV/radio & phones in rooms; complimentary afternoon tea & morning paper; evening turndown service; meeting facilities; exercise room; corporate guest program; concierge assistance
RESTRICTIONS	No pets
REVIEWED	*American Historic Bed & Breakfast Inns & Guesthouses* *America's Wonderful Little Hotels & Inns* *Best Places to Kiss in Southern California* *Best Places to Stay in California* *California Country Inns & Itineraries* *Complete Guide to Bed & Breakfasts, Inns & Guesthouses* *Country Inns & Back Roads: California* *Fodor's Bed & Breakfasts, Country Inns & Other Weekend Pleasures—* * The West Coast*
RSO	B&B 800
RATED	AAA 4 Diamonds Mobil 3 Stars

DEL MAR
(SAN DIEGO)

"The turf meets the surf" here, where wide beaches are second only to its famous thoroughbred horse racing, track-side celebrities and volatile politics. Handy to Torrey Pines State Park, natural home of the rare Torrey pine. The Southern California Exposition and National Horse Show in June and July and the Camel Grand Prix in October are major events.

THE BLUE DOOR BED & BREAKFAST

13707 Durango Dr.   Del Mar, CA 92014   (619) 755-3819
Anna Belle & Bob Schock, Resident Owners

LOCATION	Exit I-5 at Del Mar Heights Rd., west 1/4 mi. to Durango Drive, south to home on corner of Cordero Rd.
OPEN	All Year
DESCRIPTION	1971 New England Country & eclectic furnishings
NO. OF ROOMS	2-room suite w/private bath
RATES	$50-60 Reservation/cancellation policy
CREDIT CARDS	No
BREAKFAST	Full, served in dining room
AMENITIES	Private porch; TV/radio in suite; complimentary afternoon wine & cheese; limited refrigerator space & laundry facilities available; off-street parking; wedding facilities
RESTRICTIONS	No smoking. No pets. Children over 16
REVIEWED	*Annual Directory of American Bed & Breakfast* *Bed & Breakfast: Southern California* *Bed & Breakfast U.S.A*
MEMBER	Tourist Assn. of America

GULL'S NEST

12930 Via Esperia   PO Box 1056   Del Mar, CA 92014   *(619) 259-4863*
Connie & Mike Segel, Resident Owners

LOCATION	In a wooded area, 3 blocks from Torrey Pines State Beach. Ask for directions
OPEN	All Year
DESCRIPTION	1973 2-story Contemporary Wood Home Eclectic furnishings
NO. OF ROOMS	2 w/private baths
RATES	$65-85
CREDIT CARDS	No
BREAKFAST	Full, served on private decks
AMENITIES	Ocean views, king & queen beds; cable TV/radio in rooms; 1 room w/patio garden; 1 studio w/kitchen, glass-enclosed porch & separate entrance; complimentary beverages on arrival
RESTRICTIONS	No smoking. No pets (resident cat). No children
REVIEWED	*Bed & Breakfast in California* *Bed & Breakfast: Southern California* *Bed & Breakfast U.S.A.*

ROCK HAUS INN

410 15th Street   Del Mar, CA 92014   *(619) 481-3764*
Doris Holmes, Resident Owner

LOCATION	West on Del Mar Heights Rd., south on Camino Del Mar, right on 15th
OPEN	All Year
DESCRIPTION	1910 2-story Craftsman Country furnishings A former gambling parlor from prohibition days, rumored to be full of hidden passageways for the gamblers' getaways!
NO. OF ROOMS	4 w/private baths 6 share 3 baths
RATES	PB/$105-145 SB/$75-100 Reservation/cancellation policy 2-night minimum stay on summer weekends & during holidays
CREDIT CARDS	MasterCard, Visa
BREAKFAST	Continental plus, served in glassed veranda overlooking ocean
AMENITIES	Complimentary afternoon refreshments; fireplace in 1 room; radios in 4 rooms, phones in all rooms; meeting facilities
RESTRICTIONS	No smoking. No pets (resident cat). No children
REVIEWED	*American Historic Bed & Breakfast Inns & Guesthouses* *America's Wonderful Little Hotels & Inns* *Bed & Breakfast in California* *Best Places to Kiss in Southern California* *Complete Guide to Bed & Breakfasts, Inns & Guesthouses* *California Country Inns & Itineraries*
MEMBER	B&B of Southern California
RATED	AAA 2 Diamonds

DESERT HOT SPRINGS
(PALM SPRINGS)

This "Spa City" is a health resort community with its share of hot mineral springs, sports facilities and 3 golf courses. Cabot's Old Indian Pueblo & Museum is a strange 4-story home of a desert pioneer who spent 20 years building it. Just a few miles from Palm Springs.

TRAVELLER'S REPOSE

66920 First Street   PO Box 655   Desert Hot Springs, CA 92240
Marian & Sam Relkoff, Resident Owners   *(619) 329-9587*

LOCATION	East on Pierson Blvd., & north on First St.
OPEN	September 1-June 30
DESCRIPTION	1986 2-story Victorian Victorian & country furnishings
NO. OF ROOMS	1 w/private bath 2 w/shared bath
RATES	PB/$67.50-75 SB/$50-60 Reservation/cancellation policy
CREDIT CARDS	American Express
BREAKFAST	Continental plus, served in dining room
AMENITIES	Swimming pool, hot tub; parlor, complimentary afternoon tea
RESTRICTIONS	No smoking. No pets. Children over 12
REVIEWED	*American Historic Bed & Breakfast Inns & Guesthouses* *America's Wonderful Little Hotels & Inns* *Bed & Breakfast: Southern California* *Bed & Breakfast U.S.A.* *Best Places to Stay in California*

DULZURA
(SAN DIEGO CO.)

About 20 miles south of La Mesa on Hwy. 94 just north of Tecate and the Mexican border. Handy to Lake Morena State Park and fishing so good it's to keep a secret.

BROOKSIDE FARM BED & BREAKFAST INN

1373 Marron Valley Rd.   Dulzura, CA 91917   (619) 468-3043
Edd & Sally Guishard, Resident Owners

LOCATION	1/2 mi. past the Dulzura Cafe, on Hwy. 94 East
OPEN	All Year
DESCRIPTION	1926 3-story Country Farm House Eclectic furnishings
NO. OF ROOMS	6 w/private baths 2 w/shared bath 2 cabins w/private baths
RATES	PB/$55-65 SB/$45-75 Cabins/$80-85 Reservation/cancellation policy 2-night minimum stay on weekends 3-night minimum stay on some holidays
CREDIT CARDS	MasterCard, Visa
BREAKFAST	Full, served in dining room Dinner available on weekends
AMENITIES	Hot tub; fireplaces in rooms & dining room; badminton, croquet equipment available; meeting facilities; outside entrances for most rooms
RESTRICTIONS	No smoking. No pets (resident cat & farm animals). Inquire about children
AWARDS	Best Breakfast March 1991, San Diego Home & Garden 1991 Innovations Award
REVIEWED	*American Historic Bed & Breakfast Inns & Guesthouses* *America's Wonderful Little Hotels & Inns* *Bed & Breakfast in California* *Bed & Breakfast: Southern California* *Complete Guide to Bed & Breakfasts, Inns & Guesthouses* *California Country Inns & Itineraries* *Fodor's Bed & Breakfasts, Country Inns & Other Weekend Pleasures—* * The West Coast* *Inn Places for Bed & Breakfast*
MEMBER	Bed & Breakfast Innkeepers of Southern California

ENCINITAS
(SAN DIEGO)

There's blooming beauty in this "flower capital of the world," known largely for its poinsettias. But the fields of rare and exotic specimens in Quail Botanical Gardens are a visual feast. Some interesting local landmarks include the La Paloma Theater, the golden domes of the enlightening Self Realization Fellowship. Just north of Del Mar via I-5 and old Hwy. 101.

SEABREEZE BED & BREAKFAST INN

121 N. Vulcan Ave.   Encinitas, CA 92024   *(619) 944-0318*
Kirsten Richter, Resident Owner

LOCATION	Exit I-5 at Encinitas Blvd., west to Vulcan, north to Inn
OPEN	All Year
DESCRIPTION	1979 Contemporary Eclectic furnishings
NO. OF ROOMS	5 w/private baths
RATES	Sgl/$60 Dbl/$75-150 Reservation/cancellation policy 2-night minimum stay on weekends & holidays
CREDIT CARDS	Discover, MasterCard, Visa
BREAKFAST	Continental plus, served in common room or guestrooms
AMENITIES	Fireplace & phone in common room; all rooms w/TV/radio, 1 w/private hot tub, fireplace & phone; complimentary wine & cheese; meeting facilities; wedding grotto
RESTRICTIONS	No pets (resident cat)
REVIEWED	*Bed & Breakfast: Southern California* *Bed & Breakfast U.S.A.* *Complete Guide to Bed & Breakfasts, Inns & Guesthouses* *Inn Places for Bed & Breakfast*
RSO	B&B of Los Angeles

ESCONDIDO
(SAN DIEGO CO.)

Inland from the coast, about 30 miles northeast of San Diego via I-15, is the center of the county's new wine industry. Tours and tastings are plentiful. Check out Grape Day Park and Heritage Row, and dance on over to Lawrence Welk Resort Village and Dinner Theater. The city is also the main gateway to Mount Palomar Observatory and the 200-inch Hale Telescope, the world's largest.

CASTLE CREEK INN

29850 Circle R Way   Escondido, CA 92026   *(619) 751-8800*
Paul Anderson, Manager   *(800) 253-5341   FAX: (619) 751-8787*

LOCATION	Exit I-15 at East Gopher Canyon, north on Hwy. 395 to Circle R Way, east for 2 blocks
OPEN	All Year
DESCRIPTION	1980 2-story European Chalet with restaurant & tavern European furnishings
NO. OF ROOMS	30 w/private baths
RATES	$90-140 Reservation/cancellation policy
CREDIT CARDS	American Express, MasterCard, Visa
BREAKFAST	Continental plus, served in dining area Brunch, lunch & dinner available in restaurant
AMENITIES	Swimming pool; sauna; fitness studio; 2 tennis courts, golf privileges at the Castle Creek Country Club; robes, TV/radio & phones in rooms; complimentary late afternoon refreshments; meeting facilities; handicapped access
RESTRICTIONS	No smoking. No pets (resident Siamese cat, "Cassie"). No children
RATED	AAA 4 Diamonds Mobil 4 Stars

ZOSA RANCH

9381 W. Lilac Rd.   Escondido, CA 92026   (619) 723-9093
Nena Zosa, Resident Owner   Joanne Adorno, Manager   (800) 543-8803

LOCATION   Exit 15 Freeway at Pala/Oceanside, turn south on Old Hwy. 395 about
                  1-1/2 mi. to West Lilac, then left 1-1/2 mi. Ranch is on right

OPEN   All Year

DESCRIPTION   1980 Spanish Hacienda
                  On 22 acres
                  Eclectic furnishings

NO. OF ROOMS   7 w/private bath   5 w/4 shared baths
                  (Inquire about 4-bedroom guesthouse)

RATES   PB/$125-175   SB/$89-110
                  Reservation/cancellation policy
                  2-night minimum stay
                  Inquire about banquet & party rates

CREDIT CARDS   MasterCard, Visa

BREAKFAST   Full, served in dining room or on patio
                  Special meals available by arrangement

AMENITIES   Sports complex includes swimming pool, hot tub, tennis, basketball, &
                  volleyball courts; fireplace, TV/radio in family room; robes; phone
                  available; complimentary wine & cheese; outdoor grill & supplies;
                  avocado & fruit trees for the picking!

RESTRICTIONS   No smoking. No pets. Children 10 & over

REVIEWED   *Bed & Breakfast: Southern California*

FAWNSKIN
(BIG BEAR LAKE)

An upscale community on the northwest end of Big Bear Lake. Handy to everything Big Bear has to offer including Moonridge Animal Park, and Cal Tech's Solar Observatory. About 30 miles northeast of San Bernardino.

THE INN AT FAWNSKIN BED & BREAKFAST

---

880 Canyon Rd.   PO Box 378   Fawnskin, CA 92333   *(909) 866-3200*
G.B. & Susan Sneed, Resident Owners

LOCATION	3/4 mi. east of Fawnskin, directly across the road from Big Bear Lake on Hwy. 38
OPEN	All Year
DESCRIPTION	1980 2-story Custom Log Home Contemporary log furnishings
NO. OF ROOMS	2 w/private baths 2 w/shared bath
RATES	PB/$105-155 SB/$75-95 Reservation/cancellation policy 2-night minimum on weekends
CREDIT CARDS	MasterCard, Visa
BREAKFAST	Full, served in dining room Special dinners available by arrangement
AMENITIES	Jacuzzi, robes; complimentary afternoon refreshments; fireplaces in rooms & living room; baby grand piano in living room; TV/radio in rooms; game room w/pool table, wide screen TV, VCR, video library & game table; small meeting facilities. Inquire about Murder Mystery weekends
RESTRICTIONS	No smoking. No pets (resident dogs). No children
REVIEWED	*Bed & Breakfast: Southern California*
RATED	AAA 2 Diamonds

FRESNO

The heartbeat of the San Joaquin Valley, the nation's leading agricultural center —
more than a million acres of irragated land — and turkey capital of America, too.
Great things to do: the 167-acre Roeding Park and Zoo; Shin-Zen Gardens and Bird
Sanctuary in Woodland Park, and the bizzarre maze of Forestiere Underground
Gardens. Situated at the exact center of the state, 210 miles northeast of Los Angeles
via I-5 and Hwy. 99 and a straight shot to Sequoia, Kings Canyon and Yosemite
National Parks.

COUNTRY VICTORIAN

1003 S. Orange Ave.   Fresno, CA 93702　　　　　　*(209) 233-1988*
Howard & Nancy English, Resident Owners　　　　*FAX: (209) 233-3203*

LOCATION	Corner of Orange & Alta, 3 blocks south of Ventura St.
OPEN	All Year
DESCRIPTION	1900 Victorian Victorian & Country furnishings
NO. OF ROOMS	2 w/private baths 2 w/shared baths
RATES	PB/$50-75 SB/$50-65 Reservation/cancellation policy
CREDIT CARDS	No
BREAKFAST	Full, served in dining room
AMENITIES	Hot tub; TV/radio & phone in rooms; complimentary fruit basket; meeting facilities
RESTRICTIONS	No smoking. No pets
REVIEWED	*Bed & Breakfast Homes Directory: West Coast*

GARDEN GROVE

An urban Orange County community just south of Anaheim is the site of the all-glass Crystal Cathedral, TV evangelist Robert Schuller's multimillion-dollar sanctuary made of 10,000 mirrored windows. But for something down to earth, the Grove Theater Company & Festival Amphitheatre serve up outstanding entertainment.

HIDDEN VILLAGE BED & BREAKFAST

9582 Halekulani Dr.   Garden Grove, CA 92641   *(714) 636-8312*
Dick & Linda O'Berg, Resident Owners

LOCATION	10 min. south of Disneyland. Exit I-5 at Brookhurst South, south 5 mi. to Lampson, right 3 blocks to Pleasant Place, left to Halekulani Dr.
OPEN	All Year
DESCRIPTION	1950 2-Story Colonial Antique & traditional furnishings
NO. OF ROOMS	2 w/private baths 1 w/shared bath (Rooms can be combined into a suite)
RATES	PB/$45-55 SB/$50 Suite/$75 Reservation/cancellation policy
CREDIT CARDS	No
BREAKFAST	Full, served in dining room Picnic baskets available on request
AMENITIES	Robes; fireplaces & TV/radio in rooms; suite w/private sundeck; TV room w/fireplace & videos; complimentary beverages & homemade cookies; patio reception facilities
RESTRICTIONS	No smoking. No pets. Children 10 & over
REVIEWED	*Bed & Breakfast Homes Directory: West Coast* *Bed & Breakfast: Southern California* *Bed & Breakfast U.S.A.*
RSO	B&B Los Angeles Eye Openers B&B Reservations

GREEN VALLEY LAKE

Boating and fishing in the summer; back-country and downhill skiing in the winter. What more could you ask? Between Lake Arrowhead and Big Bear Lake, north of the Rim of the World Drive.

THE LODGE AT GREEN VALLEY LAKE

33655 Green Valley Lake Rd.   Green Valley Lake, CA 92341   (909) 867-4281
Gene & Margo Deshler, Resident Owners   *FAX: (909) 867-5410*

LOCATION	Close to lake & ski area. Take Hwy. 330 to Hwy. 18 east, to Green Valley Lake exit
OPEN	All Year
DESCRIPTION	1947 2-story Country Lodge with restaurant Country furnishings
NO. OF ROOMS	1 w/private bath 3 suites w/private baths and sitting areas 1 cottage w/sitting room and sink & refrigerator
RATES	$75-110 Reservation/cancellation policy 2-night minimum stay on weekends
CREDIT CARDS	MasterCard, Visa
BREAKFAST	Monday-Saturday/Continental plus Sunday/Gourmet Champagne brunch Lunch & dinner available in restaurant
AMENITIES	Parlor w/fireplace, books, games & puzzles; all rooms w/fresh flowers, sherry, TV/radio, some w/private entrances; cottage w/private entrance & patio; complimentary afternoon wine & cheese; small meeting facilities, ski shuttle stops at door
RESTRICTIONS	No smoking. No pets (resident dog & cat)
REVIEWED	*Bed & Breakfast: Southern California*
RATED	*San Bernardino Sun* Food Section 4 Stars

HANFORD

Bring a camera and walking shoes, and stay for a while. This former Southern Pacific Railroad town is a charmer of splendid Victorians and a beautifully preserved National Historic District. Not to miss: China Alley and Taoist Temple; Courthouse Square with its Classical Revival architecture, shops and antique merry-go-round; the original La Bastille jailhouse, and the wonderful Hanford Fox Theater. There are free summer concerts in the Park, the County Fair in June and in October, the Chinese Moon Festival and Renaissance Faire. Just west of Visalia, on Hwy 198 between I-5 and Hwy. 99.

THE IRWIN STREET INN

522 N. Irwin St.   Hanford, CA 93230   *(209) 583-8791*
Bruce Evans & Luci Burnworth, Managers

LOCATION	In downtown Hanford Historic District. Call for directions
OPEN	All Year
DESCRIPTION	Complex of 4 restored 2-story 1880s Victorian Homes with restaurant Antique furnishings
NO. OF ROOMS	30 w/private baths
RATES	Weekends/$79-110 Weekdays/$69-99 Reservation/cancellation policy
CREDIT CARDS	American Express, Carte Blanche, Diner's Club, MasterCard, Visa
BREAKFAST	Continental, served in restaurant or on veranda Lunch & dinner also available
AMENITIES	Swimming pool; cable TV/radio & phones in rooms; meeting & banquet facilities; limited handicapped access; off-street parking
RESTRICTIONS	Inquire about pets
REVIEWED	*American Historic Bed & Breakfast Inns & Guesthouses* *Bed & Breakfast in California* *Complete Guide to Bed & Breakfasts, Inns & Guesthouses*

HAWTHORNE

South of the L.A. metroplex between I-10 and -405. handy to Manhattan Beach and El Segundo and LAX.

DUARTE'S BED & BREAKFAST

4625 W. 131st   Hawthorne, CA 90250   *(310) 644-3795*
Maxine Duarte, Resident Owner

LOCATION	Exit Hwy. 405 at El Segundo Blvd., east to Ramona Ave., right 3 blocks to 131st
OPEN	All Year
DESCRIPTION	1976 Contemporary Contemporary furnishings
NO. OF ROOMS	1 w/private bath 1 w/shared bath
RATES	PB/$45-50 SB/$35-40
CREDIT CARDS	No
BREAKFAST	Full, served in dining room Lunch & dinner available
AMENITIES	Robes; TV/radio in rooms; exercise equipment; washer/dryer & microwave available; complimentary refreshments
RESTRICTIONS	None. Resident birds
REVIEWED	*B&B Homes Directory: West Coast*
RSO	B&B of Long Beach Eye Openers B&B Reservations Rent-A-Room International

HOLLYWOOD

Hollywood is an illusion that exists somewhere betweeen Hollywood & Vine and the Hollywood Hills. Some great reasons to come here include the Hollywood Bowl, Frank Lloyd Wright's magnificent amphitheater; Griffith Park, the second-largest city-owned park in the world (4,200 acres) includes the Griffith Observatory and Planetarium, the Greek Theater and the Los Angeles Zoo. Otherwise, the Christmas parade and the Playboy Jazz Festival are entertaining events.

ANNA'S BED & BREAKFAST

10926 Hamlin St.   North Hollywood, CA 91606 (818) 980-6191
Anna Ohler, Resident Owner FAX: (818) 549-8477

LOCATION	Ask for directions
OPEN	All Year
DESCRIPTION	1922 California/Spanish Bungalow Eclectic furnishings
NO. OF ROOMS	1 w/shared bath
RATES	Sgl/$37 Dbl/$42 Reservation/cancellation policy
CREDIT CARDS	No
BREAKFAST	Full, served in kitchen or on patio
AMENITIES	Robes, fireplace, TV/radio in room; complimentary refreshments
RESTRICTIONS	No smoking. No pets (resident dog). Children over 12
REVIEWED	*Bed & Breakfast Homes Directory: West Coast*
RSO	B&B of Los Angeles

LA MAIDA HOUSE

11159 La Maida Street   North Hollywood, CA 91601   *(818) 769-3857*
Megan Timothy, Resident Owner

LOCATION	Please call for directions
OPEN	All Year
DESCRIPTION	1926 2-Story Italian Villa Eclectic furnishings
NO. OF ROOMS	11 w/private baths In main house & bungalows
RATES	$85-210 Reservation/cancellation policy 2-night minimum stay
CREDIT CARDS	MasterCard, Visa
BREAKFAST	Continental plus, served in dining room or on patios Lunch & dinner available by prior arrangement
AMENITIES	Swimming pool, solarium, exercise room, robes; complimentary evening aperitifs and early-morning coffee & newspaper; fresh flowers; turndown service; all rooms w/fireplace, TV/radio & phones, some w/jacuzzi tubs; travel library; meeting facilities
RESTRICTIONS	No smoking. No pets (resident cats, chickens & rabbit). No children. No fur clothing
REVIEWED	*American Historic Bed & Breakfast Inns & Guesthouses* *America's Wonderful Little Hotels & Inns* *Bed & Breakfast in California* *Bed & Breakfast: Southern California* *Best Places to Stay in California* *Complete Guide to Bed & Breakfasts, Inns & Guesthouses* *Country Inns & Back Roads: California*

IDYLLWILD

A mile-high alpine resort in the spactacular San Jacinto Mountains. The performing arts are showcased year-round at The Idyllwild School of Music and the Arts. Handy to Lake Hemet and Lake Fulmore for fishing and boating. East of Los Angeles and southeast of San Bernardino via I-10 and Hwy. 243.

THE INN AT PINE COVE

23481 Hwy. 243   PO Box 2181   Idyllwild, CA 92549   *(909) 659-5033*
Lisa J. Gabriel, Resident Owner

LOCATION	3 mi. north of town on west side of Hwy. 243
OPEN	All Year
DESCRIPTION	1920/1960 A-Frame Chalets Eclectic furnishings
NO. OF ROOMS	9 w/private baths
RATES	Weekends/$80-100 Weekdays/$50-70 Reservation/cancellation policy 2-night minimum stay on weekends Inquire about minimum stay during holidays
CREDIT CARDS	American Express, MasterCard, Visa
BREAKFAST	Full, served in lodge or guestrooms
AMENITIES	Fireplace, radio, refrigerator & microwave in rooms; outside entrances; complimentary evening wine & cheese; meeting facilities; limited handicapped access
RESTRICTIONS	No smoking. No pets (resident cat)
REVIEWED	*Bed & Breakfast: Southern California (see That Special Place)* *Inn Places for Bed & Breakfast*
MEMBER	Professional Assn. of Innkeepers International

STRAWBERRY CREEK INN

26370 Hwy. 243   PO Box 1818   Idyllwild, CA 92549   (714) 659-3202
Diana Dugan & Jim Goff, Resident Owners   (800) 262-8969

LOCATION	1/4 mi. past Texaco Station
OPEN	All Year
DESCRIPTION	1941 2-Story Country House Country furnishings
NO. OF ROOMS	9 w/private baths 1 cottage w/2 baths, living room, & kitchen
RATES	Rooms/$80-95 Cottage/$125-130 Reservation/cancellation policy 2-night minimum stay in cottage 2-night minimum stay in rooms on weekends
CREDIT CARDS	MasterCard, Visa
BREAKFAST	Full, served in dining room
AMENITIES	Whirlpool tub, robes & fireplace in cottage; all rooms w/queen-size beds & radios, fireplaces in 5 rooms; complimentary wine on Saturday nights; handicapped access
RESTRICTIONS	No smoking. No pets (resident cats)
REVIEWED	*American Historic Bed & Breakfast Inns & Guesthouses* *America's Wonderful Little Hotels & Inns* *Bed & Breakfast in California* *Bed & Breakfast: Southern California* *Best Places to Stay in California* *Complete Guide to Bed & Breakfasts, Inns & Guesthouses* *Fodor's Bed & Breakfasts, Country Inns & Other Weekend Pleasures—* * The West Coast* *California Country Inns & Itineraries*
MEMBER	B&B Innkeepers of Southern California Professional Assn. of Innkeepers International
RATED	AAA 2 Diamonds

WILKUM INN BED & BREAKFAST

26770 Hwy. 243   PO Box 1115   Idyllwild, CA 92549   *(909) 659-4087*
Barbara Jones & Annamae Chambers, Resident Owners

LOCATION	At intersection of Hwy. 243 & Toll Gate Rd., 3/4 mi. south of town in Pine & Cedar forest
OPEN	All Year
DESCRIPTION	1930's 2-story shingle-sided Mountain Home Antique furnishings
NO. OF ROOMS	2 w/private bath 2 w/shared bath
RATES	PB/$65-85 SB/$55-85 Reservation/cancellation policy 2-night minimum on weekends & 3-nights during holidays Discount for multiple night stays
CREDIT CARDS	No
BREAKFAST	Continental plus, served in dining room Special meals available
AMENITIES	Robes, fresh flowers & candy in rooms; 3 rooms w/sink; phone available; river rock fireplace in common room; complimentary beverages all day & afternoon & evening snacks; small meeting facilities; limited handicapped access
RESTRICTIONS	No smoking. No pets. 2 persons per room
REVIEWED	*American Historic Bed & Breakfast Inns & Guesthouses* *Bed & Breakfast Guide California* *Bed & Breakfast Homes Directory: West Coast* *Bed & Breakfast in California* *Bed & Breakfast: Southern California* *Best Bed & Breakfasts & Country Inns: West* *Complete Guide to Bed & Breakfasts, Inns & Guesthouses* *Inn Places for Bed & Breakfast* *Non-Smoker's Guide to Bed & Breakfasts*
MEMBER	B&B Innkeepers of California Professional Assn. of Innkeepers International

INDEPENDENCE

Direct access point to the California Big Horn Sheep Zoological Area, on the east-central side of Kings Canyon and Sequoia National Parks and Inyo National Forest. Trailheads into the Park originate here and the Eastern California Museum is of interest. From Bishop, 59 miles south on Hwy. 395.

WINNEDUMAH COUNTRY INN

211 N. Edwards St. PO Box 147 Independence, CA 93526   (619) 878-2040
Alan Bergman & Marvey Chapman, Resident Owners   FAX: (619) 878-2040

LOCATION	Across from the Courthouse
OPEN	All Year
DESCRIPTION	1927 2-story Spanish Colonial with restaurant Western furnishings
NO. OF ROOMS	20 share 10 baths
RATES	SB/$37-42 Reservation/cancellation policy
CREDIT CARDS	MasterCard, Visa
BREAKFAST	Continental plus, served in dining room Lunch & dinner available
AMENITIES	TV/radio in some rooms; meeting facilities
RESTRICTIONS	No pets (resident dogs, rabbit & fish)
REVIEWED	*American Historic Bed & Breakfast Inns & Guesthouses* *The Best of the Sierra Nevada*

JULIAN
(SAN DIEGO CO.)

Everything's coming up apples in this jewel of mountain mining towns. Dozens of orchards — peach, pear and especially apples — quilt the countryside, along with Appaloosa ranches. Sample the fruits, tour the historic buildings and visit the working gold mines. Fall festivals celebrate the harvest and wildflowers celebrate spring. From Escondido, 34 miles southeast via Hwy. 78.

THE ARTISTS' LOFT

4811 Pine Ridge Ave.   PO Box 2408   Julian, CA 92036   *(619) 765-0765*
Chuck & Nanessence Kimball, Resident Artists

LOCATION	In Pine Hills area (map sent w/reservation confirmation)
OPEN	All Year
DESCRIPTION	1961 Ranch Contemporary furnishings
NO. OF ROOMS	2 w/private baths
RATES	$95 Reservation/cancellation policy Inquire about minimum stay
CREDIT CARDS	No
BREAKFAST	Full, served in dining area of kitchen or courtyard
AMENITIES	Wood burning stoves, private entrances & queen beds in rooms; complimentary coffee & tea; handicapped access
RESTRICTIONS	No smoking. No pets (resident cats). No children
MEMBER	Julian B&B Guild

BUTTERFIELD BED & BREAKFAST

2284 Sunset Dr.   PO Box 1115   Julian, CA 92036   *(619) 765-2179*
Ray & Mary Trimmins, Resident Owners   *FAX: (619) 765-1115*

LOCATION	1 mi. east of town. From Hwy. 78, turn right on Whispering Pines then right on Sunset
OPEN	All Year
DESCRIPTION	1940 Country House Antique & Country furnishings
NO. OF ROOMS	4 w/private baths 1 cottage w/private bath
RATES	$79-125 Reservation/cancellation policy 2-night minimum stay Sept.-Jan.
CREDIT CARDS	MasterCard, Visa
BREAKFAST	Full, served in dining room or gazebo Romantic dinners available
AMENITIES	Garden gazebo; robes; fireplaces & TV/radio in rooms; complimentary afternoon refreshments; guest kitchen in game room; wedding facilities; horse-drawn carriage rides available; inquire about anniversary & birthday specials
RESTRICTIONS	No smoking. No pets (resident cats). Inquire about children
REVIEWED	*Best Places to Kiss in Southern California* *Complete Guide to Bed & Breakfasts, Inns & Guesthouses*
MEMBER	Julian B&B Guild

EVENSTAR LODGE BED & BREAKFAST

4696 Evenstar Ln.   PO Box 1558   Julian, CA 92036   *(619) 765-1860*
Donald L. McCarty, Resident Owner   *FAX: (619) 765-0868*

LOCATION	In wooded area 5 mi. southwest of town: Go 1 mi. west on Hwy. 78, south 3 mi. on Pine Hills Rd. to Blue Jay, past Pine Hills Lodge to Luneta, then 1 mi. to Evenstar
OPEN	All Year
DESCRIPTION	1986 2-story log & stone house Some antique & eclectic furnishings Cathedral ceilings
NO. OF ROOMS	1 w/private bath 2 w/shared bath
RATES	PB/$85 SB/$70 Reservation/cancellation policy
CREDIT CARDS	No
BREAKFAST	Full, served in common room or on deck
AMENITIES	Large deck; TV/radio in rooms; TV/VCR & fire-view wood burning stove in common room; one room w/fireplace stove & whirlpool bath
RESTRICTIONS	No smoking. No pets (resident cats & dog)

HOMESTEAD BED & BREAKFAST

4924 Hwy. 79   PO Box 1208   Julian, CA 92036   *(619) 765-1536*
Dick & Mary Ellen Thilken, Resident Owners

LOCATION	4-1/2 mi. south of town on Hwy. 79
OPEN	All Year (Closed Thanksgiving & Christmas)
DESCRIPTION	1979 2-story Lodge Country furnishings
NO. OF ROOMS	2 w/private baths 2 w/shared baths
RATES	PB/$85-95 SB/$80-85 Reservation/cancellation policy 2-night minimum September-December & during holiday weekends
CREDIT CARDS	No
BREAKFAST	Full, served in dining room or on patio
	Special meals available on request
AMENITIES	Robes, king beds; 2-story fireplace; game table & forest views in common room; complimentary afternoon refreshments & evening dessert; small meeting facilities, handicapped access
RESTRICTIONS	No smoking. No pets (resident dog)
REVIEWED	*Bed & Breakfast: Southern California*
MEMBER	Julian B&B Guild

JULIAN GOLD RUSH HOTEL

2032 Main St.   PO Box 1856   Julian, CA 92036
Steve & Gig Ballinger, Resident Owners

(619) 765-0201
(800) 734-5854

LOCATION	Corner of Main & B Streets
OPEN	All Year
DESCRIPTION	1897 2-story Victorian Victorian furnishings National Historic Register
NO. OF ROOMS	5 w/private baths 13 w/shared baths
RATES	PB/$76-145 SB/$38-82 Reservation/cancellation policy Inquire about minimum stay on weekends
CREDIT CARDS	American Express, MasterCard, Visa
BREAKFAST	Full, served in dining room
AMENITIES	Fireplace in 1 room; radio in 2 rooms; books, games & wood stove in lobby; complimentary afternoon tea; meeting facilities
RESTRICTIONS	No pets
REVIEWED	*Bed & Breakfast in California* *Bed & Breakfast: Southern California* *Best Places to Stay in California* *California Country Inns & Itineraries* *Fodor's Bed & Breakfasts, Country Inns & Other Weekend Pleasures— The West Coast*
MEMBER	Bed & Breakfast Innkeepers of Southern California

JULIAN WHITE HOUSE
BED & BREAKFAST INN

3014 Blue Jay Dr.   PO Box 824   Julian, CA 92036   *(619) 765-1764*
Mary & Alan Marvin, Resident Owners

LOCATION	West on Hwy. 78 to Pine Hills Rd., south 2 mi. to Blue Jay
OPEN	All Year
DESCRIPTION	1978 2-story columned Petite Colonial Victorian furnishings
NO. OF ROOMS	2 w/private baths 2 w/shared baths
RATES	PB/$100-107 SB/$90 Reservation/cancellation policy 2-night minimum stay
CREDIT CARDS	MasterCard, Visa
BREAKFAST	Full, served in dining room
AMENITIES	Sitting/music room w/marble fireplace; robes; complimentary evening desserts
RESTRICTIONS	No smoking. No pets (resident cats)
REVIEWED	*Best Places to Kiss in Southern California* *California Country Inns & Itineraries*
MEMBER	Julian B&B Guild

THE LEELIN WIKIUP BED & BREAKFAST

1645 Whispering Pines Dr. PO Box 2363 Julian, CA 92036   (619) 765-1890
Lee & Linda Stanley, Resident Owners

LOCATION	1-1/2 mi. east of town on Hwy. 78, right on Whispering Pines, 1st driveway on left
OPEN	All Year
DESCRIPTION	1981 wood mountain lodge Eclectic furnishings
NO. OF ROOMS	2 w/private baths
RATES	$85 Reservation/cancellation policy 2-night minimum stay on weekends
CREDIT CARDS	To guarantee reservation, prefer cash or check
BREAKFAST	Full gourmet, served in dining room Special meals available w/advance notice
AMENITIES	Fireplace in dining room; radio in rooms; complimentary refreshments
RESTRICTIONS	No smoking. Inquire about pets (resident cats & dogs). Inquire about children
MEMBER	Julian B&B Guild

MOUNTAIN HIGH BED & BREAKFAST

4110 Deer Lake Rd.   PO Box 268   Julian, CA 92036   *(619) 765-1083*
Carol Pike, Resident Owner

LOCATION	3 mi. west of town on Hwy. 78 to Pine Hills Rd., 1 mi. to Deer Lake Park Rd.
OPEN	All Year
DESCRIPTION	1950 Country Ranch French Country furnishings
NO. OF ROOMS	1 w/private bath 1 cottage w/private bath
RATES	Room/$95 Cottage/$105 Reservation/cancellation policy 2-night minimum on weekends
CREDIT CARDS	MasterCard, Visa
BREAKFAST	Full, served in guestroom & cottage Special dinners available
AMENITIES	Private decks & garden patio; fireplaces, TV/VCR/radio in cottage, TV/radio in room; complimentary refreshments
RESTRICTIONS	No smoking. No pets. No children
REVIEWED	*Bed & Breakfast: Southern California* *Best Places to Kiss in Southern California* *The Definitive California Bed & Breakfast Vacation & Touring Guide*
MEMBER	Julian B&B Guild

PINECROFT MANOR

2142 Whispering Pines Dr.   PO Box 665   Julian, CA 92036   (619) 765-1611
Diane Boyer, Resident Owner

LOCATION	1.5 mi. east of center of town, on Hwy. 78, in Whispering Pines
OPEN	All Year
DESCRIPTION	1979 5-level English Tudor with 30' cathedral ceilings Antique furnishings
NO. OF ROOMS	2 w/shared baths
RATES	Rooms/$89 Reservation/cancellation policy 2-night minimum stay on holiday weekends
CREDIT CARDS	MasterCard, Visa
BREAKFAST	Full, served in dining room
AMENITIES	Robes; fireplace in parlor; complimentary evening refreshments; private decks
RESTRICTIONS	No smoking. Children 12 & over in manor. Children & pets OK in cabin (resident cats & dog)
REVIEWED	*Bed & Breakfast: Southern California*
RSO	Back Country Tours
MEMBER	Julian B&B Guild

RANDOM OAKS RANCH
BED & BREAKFAST

3742 Pine Hills Rd.   PO Box 454   Julian, CA 92036   *(619) 765-1094*
Gene & Shari Helsel, Resident Owners

LOCATION	From Hwy. 78/79, take Pine Hills Rd. for 1 mi. to white 3-rail fence & sign
OPEN	All Year
DESCRIPTION	2 private cottages remodeled in 1992 & 1993 Elegant eclectic furnishings On Thoroughbred ranch
NO. OF ROOMS	2 cottages w/private baths
RATES	$139-159 Reservation/cancellation policy 2-night minimum on weekends
CREDIT CARDS	MasterCard, Visa
BREAKFAST	Full, delivered to cottages Romantic picnics available at extra charge
AMENITIES	Private jacuzzis; fireplaces; complimentary bottle of wine on arrival; coffee, tea, hot chocolate & cider
RESTRICTIONS	No smoking. Inquire about pets (resident horses, dogs & cat). Children over 14
REVIEWED	*Best Places to Kiss in Southern California*
MEMBER	Julian B&B Guild

SHADOW MOUNTAIN RANCH
BED & BREAKFAST

2771 Frisius Rd.   Box 791   Julian, CA 92036   *(619) 765-0323*
Jim & Loretta Ketcherside, Resident Owners

LOCATION	West of town on Hwy. 78-79, south on Pine Hills Rd., 2 mi. to sign, left 1 block
OPEN	All Year
DESCRIPTION	1940 Ranch Eclectic furnishings (theme rooms)
NO. OF ROOMS	1 w/shared bath 4 cottages w/private baths 1 tree house w/half bath (shower in main house)
RATES	$70-100 Reservation/cancellation policy 2-night minimum on weekends
CREDIT CARDS	No
BREAKFAST	Full, served in Apple Pantry (separate gathering room) Inquire about special meals
AMENITIES	Lap pool, hot tub, robes; wood-burning stoves & TV/radio in rooms; complimentary afternoon refreshments; meeting facilities; handicapped access
RESTRICTIONS	No smoking. No pets (resident dog, cows, horses & goats). No children
REVIEWED	*Bed & Breakfast in California* *Bed & Breakfast: Southern California* *Best Places to Kiss in Southern California* *Best Places to Stay in California*
MEMBER	Julian B&B Guild

VILLA IDALEEN BED & BREAKFAST

2609 D Street   PO Box 190   Julian, CA 92036   (619) 765-1252
Idalene Potter, Resident Owner

LOCATION	In residential area, center of town
OPEN	All Year
DESCRIPTION	1981 2-story Contemporary Victorian Antique furnishings
NO. OF ROOMS	1 w/private bath 2 w/shared bath
RATES	PB/$85 SB/$65-75 Reservation/cancellation policy 2-night minimum stay in room w/private bath
CREDIT CARDS	No
BREAKFAST	Full, served in dining room
AMENITIES	Swimming pool, hot tub; radios in all rooms, 1 w/fireplace & handicapped access
RESTRICTIONS	No smoking. No pets
REVIEWED	*Bed & Breakfast: Southern California*
MEMBER	Julian B&B Guild

KERNVILLE

The town's location says it all: In the Kern River Valley, at the south central end of Sequoia National Forest, on the Wild and Scenic Kern River and at the north edge of Lake Isabella. This is the jumping-off place for whitewater rafting, boating, waterskiing, fishing and exploring the home of the giant sequoia. There's a golf course, too. Check out the annual Whitewater Race in April, the Summer Festival and Sailboat Regatta in September and Kernville Stampede in October. North of Bakersfield via Hwys. 178 and 155.

KERN RIVER INN BED & BREAKFAST

119 Kern River Dr.   PO Box 1725   Kernville, CA 93238   *(619) 376-6750*
Mike Meehan & Marti Andrews, Resident Owners

LOCATION	Inn faces the Kern River & Riverside Park
OPEN	All Year
DESCRIPTION	1990 2-story farmhouse with wrap-around porches Country furnishings
NO. OF ROOMS	6 w/private baths
RATES	Sgl/$59-79 Dbl/$69-89 Reservation/cancellation policy Inquire about minimum stay during summer, holidays & special events
CREDIT CARDS	MasterCard, Visa
BREAKFAST	Full, served in dining room
AMENITIES	All rooms w/river views, king or queen beds, & radios, some have fireplaces & jacuzzi tubs; complimentary afternoon & evening refreshments; small meeting facilities; limited handicapped access, airport pick-up service
RESTRICTIONS	No smoking. No pets. Children over 12
REVIEWED	*The Annual Directory of American Bed & Breakfasts* *Bed & Breakfast in California* *Bed & Breakfast: Southern California* *Complete Guide to Bed & Breakfasts, Inns & Guesthouses*
MEMBER	National B&B Assn. Professional Assn. of Innkeepers International
RATED	AAA 3 Diamonds Mobil 2 Stars

THE NEILL HOUSE

100 Tobias St.   PO Box 1018   Kernville, CA 93238-1018   (619) 376-2771
Dawn Jordan, Manager   FAX: (619) 376-4848

LOCATION	At corner of Tobias & Scodie
OPEN	All Year (Closed 1/5-2/5)
DESCRIPTION	1890 2-story Victorian Farmhouse Late Victorian furnishings
NO. OF ROOMS	2 w/private baths 2 w/shared bath
RATES	PB/$110-135 SB/$95 Reservation/cancellation policy
CREDIT CARDS	American Express, MasterCard, Visa
BREAKFAST	Full formal, served in dining room Continental served in guestroom or to go
AMENITIES	Robes; clawfoot tubs; down comforters; parlor w/player piano & fireplace; TV/radio in some rooms; complimentary wine & cheese and refreshments on arrival; meeting facilities; lavish High Tea by reservation only
RESTRICTIONS	Smoking limited. No pets
REVIEWED	*Bed & Breakfast: Southern California*

WHISPERING PINES LODGE
BED & BREAKFAST

13745 Sierra Way   Rt. 1, Box 41   Kernville, CA 93238   *(619) 376-2334*
Linda Ramos, Manager   *FAX: (619) 376-3735*

LOCATION	Kernville Rd. to Sierra Way, left 3/10 mi. Lodge is on left side
OPEN	All Year
DESCRIPTION	1945 Lodge w/Riverview Bungalows & Country Cottages Country furnishings On the Kern River
NO. OF ROOMS	11 w/private baths
RATES	$79-129 Reservation/cancellation policy 2-night minimum on weekends
CREDIT CARDS	American Express, Diner's Club, MasterCard, Visa
BREAKFAST	Full gourmet, served in dining room
AMENITIES	Swimming pool w/1000 sq. ft. deck overlooking Kern River, hot tub; fireplaces in 7 rooms; TV/HBO/VCR'S/radio, phones, compact refrigerator, complimentary candy & gourmet coffee in rooms; meeting, wedding & reunion facilities; copy & FAX machines available
RESTRICTIONS	No smoking. No pets
RSO	Kern Valley/Lake Isabella Hotel/Motel Assn. (800-628-6957)
RATED	AAA 3 Diamonds Mobil Quality Rated

KINGS CANYON

Great cross-country skiing in Kings Canyon National Park, just 75 miles east of Fresno.

MONTECITO-SEQUOIA LODGE

8000 General's Hwy. PO Box 858   *(209) 565-3388*
Kings Canyon, CA 93633   *(800) 227-9900*
Virginia Barnes, Owner   Scott Stowers, Manager   *FAX: (209) 565-3223*

LOCATION	2 mi. past Kings Canyon National Park entrance, right at "Y", then 8 mi. south
OPEN	September-June
DESCRIPTION	1969-75 Mountain Lodge Rustic alpine furnishings
NO. OF ROOMS	35 w/private baths
RATES	Sgl/$95 Dbl/$138 Reservation/cancellation policy
CREDIT CARDS	American Express, MasterCard, Visa
BREAKFAST	Full, served in dining room Dinner also included in rate Lunch & special holiday meals available
AMENITIES	Swimming pool, hot tub; fireplace in common room; complimentary refreshments; meeting facilities
RESTRICTIONS	No pets (resident pet). Inquire about children
AWARDS	Top 10 Cross-Country Ski Lodges in the Far West—1992, Snow Country
REVIEWED	*Complete Guide to Bed & Breakfasts, Inns & Guesthouses*
MEMBER	American B&B Assn.
RATED	AAA Approved

Laguna Beach

The ultimate California beach town and artist's colony, bordered by ocean bluffs, narrow streets, powder-sand beaches and secluded inlets. The major summer event, it's famous Festival of Arts and Pageant of the Masters, is a 7-week summer concoction of exhibits, ballets, chorales and the Pageant's living tableaux. South of Long Beach on the Pacific Coast Highway.

The Carriage House

1322 Catalina St. Laguna Beach, CA 92651　　　　　　*(714) 494-8945*
Dee & Tom Taylor, Resident Owners

LOCATION	Exit Pacific Coast Hwy. at Cress, continue to Catalina
OPEN	All Year
DESCRIPTION	1920 2-story Colonial Inn Antique furnishings Laguna Beach Historic Register
NO. OF ROOMS	6 suites w/private baths
RATES	$95-150 Reservation/cancellation policy 2-night minimum stay on weekends 3-night minimum stay during holidays
CREDIT CARDS	No
BREAKFAST	Continental plus, served in Grandma Bean's Dining Room
AMENITIES	TV/radio & sitting room in suites & most have kitchens; complimentary wine, cheese, fruit & candy; small meeting facilities; reserved parking
RESTRICTIONS	No pets (resident cat)
AWARDS	Best B&B In Laguna, 1990
REVIEWED	*American Historic Bed & Breakfast Inns & Guesthouses* *America's Wonderful Little Hotels & Inns* *Annual Directory of American Bed & Breakfast* *Bed & Breakfast Guest Houses & Inns of America* *Bed & Breakfast in California* *Bed & Breakfast: Southern California* *California Country Inns & Itineraries* *Complete Guide to Bed & Breakfasts, Inns & Guesthouses*
RSO	Bed & Breakfast 800
MEMBER	B&B Innkeepers of Southern California California Hotel/Motel Assn. Hospitality Assn. of Laguna Beach
RATED	AAA 2 Diamonds

CASA LAGUNA INN

2510 S. Coast Highway   Laguna Beach, CA 92651   (714) 494-2996
Ted & Louise Gould, Resident Owners   FAX: (714) 494-5009

LOCATION	Exit Freeways 5 or 405 at Laguna Canyon Rd., west to Pacific Coast Hwy., south 1-1/2 mi.
OPEN	All Year
DESCRIPTION	1940's Spanish Antique & eclectic furnishings
NO. OF ROOMS	15 w/private baths, 4 suites w/private baths, kitchens & balconies 1-bedroom cottage, & 1-bedroom Mission House w/private baths
RATES	$105-225 Reservation/cancellation policy
CREDIT CARDS	American Express, Discover, MasterCard, Visa
BREAKFAST	Continental plus, served in library
AMENITIES	Ocean view; heated swimming pool & deck; library; all rooms w/TV/radio, phones, decks or balconies; fireplaces in cottage & Mission House; complimentary afternoon tea & wine; small meeting & special event facilities; limited handicapped access
RESTRICTIONS	No pets (resident cat)
REVIEWED	*American Historic Bed & Breakfast Inns & Guesthouses* *America's Wonderful Little Hotels & Inns* *Bed & Breakfast in California* *Bed & Breakfast: Southern California* *Complete Guide to Bed & Breakfasts, Inns & Guesthouses* *Inn Places for Bed & Breakfast*
RSO	Bed & Breakfast 800
RATED	AAA 2 Diamonds

EILER'S INN

741 S. Coast Highway   Laguna Beach, CA 92651   *(714) 494-3004*
Annette & Henrik Wirtz, Owners   *Jonna Iversen, Manager*

LOCATION	Hwy. 405 Exit 133 to Pacific Coast Hwy., left to Cleo, right on Cleo to G'Auidta, left to Inn
OPEN	All Year
DESCRIPTION	1940 2-story New Orleans Antique furnishings
NO. OF ROOMS	11 w/private baths 1 suite w/private bath & kitchen
RATES	Rooms/$80-170 Suite/$175 Reservation/cancellation policy 2-night minimum on weekends
CREDIT CARDS	American Express, MasterCard, Visa
BREAKFAST	Continental plus, served in living room or courtyard
AMENITIES	Courtyard; sun deck w/ocean view; fresh flowers, fruit & candy in all rooms, fireplace in 1 room; complimentary champagne on arrival, tea & coffee all day, & evening wine & cheese in courtyard; live classical guitar music on Saturdays; small meeting facilities, limited handicapped access
RESTRICTIONS	No pets
REVIEWED	*American Historic Bed & Breakfast Inns & Guesthouses* *America's Wonderful Little Hotels & Inns* *Bed & Breakfast in California* *Bed & Breakfast: Southern California* *Best Places to Stay in California* *California Country Inns & Itineraries* *The Christian Bed & Breakfast Directory* *Complete Guide to Bed & Breakfasts, Inns & Guesthouses* *Fodor's Bed & Breakfasts, Country Inns & Other Weekend Pleasures—* *The West Coast* *Inn Places for Bed & Breakfast* *Inspected, Rated & Approved Bed & Breakfasts*
MEMBER	American B&B Assn.
RATED	AAA 2 Diamonds ABBA 3 Crowns Mobil 3 Stars

HOTEL FIRENZE

1289 S. Coast Highway   Laguna Beach, Ca 92651   *(714) 497-2446*
Karen McMaugh, Manager

LOCATION	12 blocks south of Laguna Freeway 133
OPEN	All Year
DESCRIPTION	1927 2-story Mediterranean Revival Antique furnishings Laguna Beach Historic Register
NO. OF ROOMS	16 w/private baths 4 suites w/private baths
RATES	$60-160 Reservation/cancellation policy 2-night minimum stay on weekends 3-night minimum stay during holidays
CREDIT CARDS	MasterCard, Visa
BREAKFAST	Continental plus, served in breakfast room or courtyard
AMENITIES	Fireplace in lobby; rooftop deck; small meeting facilities
RESTRICTIONS	No smoking. Resident cat
REVIEWED	*Bed & Breakfast: Southern California*
MEMBER	American B&B Assn. California Assn. of B&B Inns

INN AT LAGUNA BEACH

211 N. Pacific Coast Hwy.   Laguna Beach, CA 92651   (714) 497-9722
Adrianne Beck, Manager   (800) 544-4479   FAX: (714) 497-9972

LOCATION	On oceanfront. Exit Hwy. 5 at Hwy. 133, south to town, right on Pacific Coast Hwy., 1st building on left
OPEN	All Year
DESCRIPTION	1990 Mediterranean California casual furnishings
NO. OF ROOMS	70 w/private baths
RATES	$99-299 Reservation/cancellation policy Inquire about minimum stay on weekends & holidays
CREDIT CARDS	American Express, Carte Blanche, Diner's Club, Visa
BREAKFAST	Continental, served in guestrooms
AMENITIES	Swimming pool, hot tub, robes; TV/radio, phones & mini refrigerators in rooms; complimentary morning newspaper; meeting facilities; handicapped access
RESTRICTIONS	No pets
REVIEWED	*America's Wonderful Little Hotels & Inns*
RATED	AAA 3 Diamonds Mobil 3 Stars

LA JOLLA
(SAN DIEGO)

In Spanish it means "the jewel," which says it all. The 7-mile Rivera-like coast is the main attraction of this very upscale, elegant playground. But this is also a noted center for research that includes the Scripps Institute of Oceanography and the Salk Institute. On the light side, sideslip on over to the Torrey Pines Glider Port overlooking infamous Black's Beach; the museum of Contemporary Art; La Jolla Caves, and the best beaches on the north end of town.

THE BED & BREAKFAST INN AT LA JOLLA

7753 Draper Ave.   La Jolla, CA 92037   (619) 456-2066
Pierrette Tummerman, Manager   FAX: (619) 453-4487

LOCATION	Exit I-5 at Ardath Rd., go west to Torrey Pines Rd., left to Kline St., right for 4 blocks, right on Draper
OPEN	All Year
DESCRIPTION	1913 Cubist designed by Irving Gill Elegant country furnishings Original gardens designed by famed horticulturist Kate Sessions San Diego Historic Register
NO. OF ROOMS	15 w/private baths 1 w/shared bath (10 in main house, 6 in annex)
RATES	PB/$100-225 SB/$85 Reservation/cancellation policy 2-night minimum on weekends
CREDIT CARDS	MasterCard, Visa
BREAKFAST	Continental plus, served in dining room, guest rooms, garden or on sundeck
AMENITIES	Fresh fruit, sherry, fresh flowers & terry robes in all rooms; some rooms w/fireplaces, TV's, phones & refrigerators; complimentary afternoon wine & cheese; small meeting facilities; garden, deck & library sitting room; handicapped access
RESTRICTIONS	No smoking. No pets. Children over 7
REVIEWED	*American Historic Bed & Breakfast Inns & Guesthouses* *America's Wonderful Little Hotels & Inns* *Bed & Breakfast in California* *Bed & Breakfast: Southern California* *Best Places to Stay in California* *Complete Guide to Bed & Breakfasts, Inns & Guesthouses* *California Country Inns & Itineraries*
RSO	California Riviera 800
RATED	Mobil 3 Stars

COSTELLO'S BED & BREAKFAST

(RSO)   *Reservations: (415) 696-1690   FAX: (415) 696-1699*

LOCATION	On the Avenida de la Playa
OPEN	All Year
DESCRIPTION	1960s Eichler Contemporary Elegant furnishings
NO. OF ROOMS	1 w/private bath
RATES	$70 Reservation/cancellation policy 2-night minimum stay
CREDIT CARDS	MasterCard, Visa
BREAKFAST	Full gourmet, served in dining area
AMENITIES	TV/radio in room
RESTRICTIONS	No smoking. No pets (resident cat)
RSO	B&B International

PROSPECT PARK INN

1110 Prospect St.   La Jolla, CA 92037   (619) 454-0133   (800) 433-1609
Jean Beazley, Manager   FAX: (619) 454-1056

LOCATION	Follow signs into town, right turn on Prospect St.
OPEN	All Year
DESCRIPTION	1950 Red Brick Contemporary furnishings
NO. OF ROOMS	22 w/private baths
RATES	$79-129 Reservation/cancellation policy 2-night minimum stay during holidays
CREDIT CARDS	American Express, Diner's Club, Discover, MasterCard, Visa
BREAKFAST	Continental plus, served in guest room or on sundeck
AMENITIES	TV/radio, phones, coffee makers & hair dryers in rooms; complimentary refreshments
RESTRICTIONS	No smoking. No pets
RATED	AAA 2 Diamonds

SCRIPPS INN

555 Coast Blvd. South La Jolla, CA 92037	*(619) 454-3391*
Charlene Browne, Manager	*FAX: (619) 459-6758*

LOCATION	From I-5 South, right on La Jolla Village Dr., left on Torrey Pines 1.5 mi., right on Prospect, right on Cuvier
OPEN	All Year
DESCRIPTION	1948 Lodge on the ocean Country furnishings
NO. OF ROOMS	13 w/private baths & ocean views
RATES	$80-165 Reservation/cancellation policy 2-night minimum stay on weekends
CREDIT CARDS	American Express, MasterCard, Visa
BREAKFAST	Continental, served on upper lanai
AMENITIES	Fireplaces & kitchenettes in suites; all rooms have TV, phone & refrigerator, handicapped access
RESTRICTIONS	None. Resident cat
RATED	AAA 2 Diamonds

STOERMER'S BED & BREAKFAST

(RSO)	*Reservations: (415) 696-1690 FAX: (415) 696-1699*

LOCATION	On Candlelight Drive
OPEN	All Year
DESCRIPTION	1970s Plantation Style Classic furnishings
NO. OF ROOMS	2 w/private baths
RATES	$65-75 Reservation/cancellation policy 2-night minimum
CREDIT CARDS	MasterCard, Visa
BREAKFAST	Full, served in dining room or poolside
AMENITIES	Swimming pool, hot tub; TV/radio in rooms
RESTRICTIONS	No smoking. No pets
RSO	B&B International

LAKE ARROWHEAD

High in the San Bernardino Mountains, this small and pretty year-round alpine retreat is a highlight of the scenic Rim of the World Drive. Skiing and water sports are the main agenda. In summer, tour the lake aboard the Arrowhead Queen for a view of the exclusive North Shore. Heaps Park Arboretum is a visual feast.

BLUEBELLE HOUSE BED & BREAKFAST

263 S. State Hwy. 173   PO Box 2177   Lake Arrowhead, CA 92352
Rick & Lila Peiffer, Resident Owners   *(909) 336-3292*

LOCATION	2/10 mi. from village traffic light
OPEN	All Year
DESCRIPTION	1958 European European furnishings
NO. OF ROOMS	3 w/private baths 2 w/shared bath
RATES	PB/$95-110 SB/$75 Reservation/cancellation policy 2-night minimum on weekends
CREDIT CARDS	MasterCard, Visa
BREAKFAST	Full, served in dining room
AMENITIES	Complimentary wine & cheese; small meeting facilities
RESTRICTIONS	No smoking. No pets. No children
REVIEWED	*American Historic Bed & Breakfast Inns & Guesthouses* *Annual Directory of American Bed & Breakfast* *Bed & Breakfast in California* *Bed & Breakfast North America* *Bed & Breakfast: Southern California* *Christian Bed & Breakfast Directory* *Complete Guide to Bed & Breakfasts, Inns & Guesthouses* *Country Inns of the Far West: California* *Fodor's Bed & Breakfast Guide*
RATED	AAA 3 Diamonds

THE CARRIAGE HOUSE BED & BREAKFAST

472 Emerald Dr.   PO Box 982   Lake Arrowhead, CA 92352   (909) 336-1400
Lee & Johan Karstens, Resident Owners

LOCATION	From Village entrance, 2.2 mi. northwest on Hwy. 173 to Emerald Dr.
OPEN	All Year
DESCRIPTION	1956 New England Country House Country furnishings
NO. OF ROOMS	3 w/private baths
RATES	$95-120 Reservation/cancellation policy 2-night minimum stay on weekends Inquire about minimum stays during holidays
CREDIT CARDS	Discover, MasterCard, Visa
BREAKFAST	Full/Weekends Continental/Weekdays Served in dining room
AMENITIES	All rooms w/lake views, down comforters, & TV/radios; complimentary afternoon refreshments & wine & hors d'oeuvres, & bedtime treat
RESTRICTIONS	No smoking. No pets (resident dog & parrot). No children
REVIEWED	*Annual Directory of American Bed & Breakfast* *Bed & Breakfast Homes Directory: West Coast* *Bed & Breakfast: Southern California* *Christian Bed & Breakfast Directory* *Complete Guide to Bed & Breakfasts, Inns & Guesthouses* *Inn Places for Bed & Breakfast*

CHATEAU DU LAC

911 Hospital Rd.   PO Box 1098   Lake Arrowhead, CA 92352
Oscar & Jody Wilson, Resident Owners   (909) 337-6488 FAX: (909) 337-6746

LOCATION	Next to Mountains Community Hospital. From stoplight in village, 3 mi. on Hwy. 173 to Hospital Rd., turn right, go up hill to first house on the right
OPEN	All Year
DESCRIPTION	1986 3-story Victorian French Country furnishings
NO. OF ROOMS	4 w/private baths 2 w/shared bath
RATES	$95-250 Reservation/cancellation policy 2-night minimum on weekends
CREDIT CARDS	American Express, Discover, MasterCard, Visa
BREAKFAST	Full, served in dining room Dinner & special meals available on request
AMENITIES	All rooms have queen beds, TVs & phones, 2 have fireplaces, some have private entrances, terraces or balconies, & Jacuzzi tubs; library; game table in living room; complimentary afternoon tea; meeting/party facilities
RESTRICTIONS	No smoking. No pets (resident dog). Children over 14
REVIEWED	*Annual Directory of American Bed & Breakfast* *Best Places to Kiss in Southern California* *Best Places to Stay in California* *California Country Inns & Itineraries*

EAGLE'S LANDING

27706 Cedarwood   Lake Arrowhead, CA   (909) 336-2642
Mailing address: PO Box 1510   Blue Jay, CA 92317
Dorothy & Jack Stone, Resident Owners

LOCATION	On the West Shore. From 3-way stop in Blue Jay, left on North Bay Rd. to corner of North Bay & Cedarwood
OPEN	All Year
DESCRIPTION	1982 3-story Mountain Gothic Antique & eclectic furnishings
NO. OF ROOMS	3 w/private baths 1 suite w/private bath, sitting room & full bar
RATES	Rooms/$95-125 Suite/$175 Reservation/cancellation policy 2-night minimum stay on weekends 3-night minimum stay during major holidays
CREDIT CARDS	Discover, MasterCard, Visa
BREAKFAST	Full, served in breakfast room Sunday brunch served in Hunt Room Christmas dinners available
AMENITIES	All rooms w/king & queen beds, robes & radios, 1 w/private deck; suite w/fireplace, TV/stereo, refrigerator & private deck; complimentary evening refreshments; meeting facilities, lake privileges
RESTRICTIONS	No smoking. No pets. No children
REVIEWED	America's Wonderful Little Hotels & Inns Annual Directory of American Bed & Breakfast Bed & Breakfast Homes Directory: West Coast Bed & Breakfast: Southern California California Country Inns & Itineraries Complete Guide to Bed & Breakfasts, Inns & Guesthouses Inn Places for Bed & Breakfast

PROPHETS' PARADISE

26845 Modoc Lane   PO Box 2116   Lake Arrowhead, CA 92352
LaVerne & Tom Prophet, Resident Owners   *(909) 336-1969*

LOCATION	From Blue Jay Turnoff, left on Hwy. 189, right on Grass Valley Rd., left on Golf Course Rd., left on Oakmont, left on Brentwood, right on Trinity, left on Modor Ln. to green awning
OPEN	All Year
DESCRIPTION	1983 Mountain Tudor Antique furnishings
NO. OF ROOMS	2 suites w/private baths 1 room w/private bath
RATES	$90-160 Reservation/cancellation policy 2-night minimum on weekends
CREDIT CARDS	MasterCard, Visa
BREAKFAST	Full, served in dining room, on the decks, or in suite
AMENITIES	Fireplace & TV/VCR in living room; game room w/pooltable; suites have decks w/private entrances, wet bars & TV/VCR, 1 has private spa; complimentary evening hors d'oeuvres
RESTRICTIONS	No smoking. No pets (resident dog & cats). Inquire about children
REVIEWED	*Bed & Breakfast: Southern California*

LAKE HUGHES

Horse trails, mountain bike trails, an 18 hole golf course and also Lake Elizabeth; all in the San Gabriel Mountains. Not a bad place to disappear to.

LAKE HUGHES TRADING POST & ROCK INN

17539 Elizabeth Lake Rd.   PO Box 407   Lake Hughes, CA 93532
Paul Koslo, Resident Owner   *(805) 724-1855*

LOCATION	1 mi. east of stop sign at junction of Lake Hughes Rd. & Elizabeth Lake Rd.
OPEN	All Year (Closed Christmas)
DESCRIPTION	1929 2-story River rock Inn with restaurant & bar Period antique furnishings
NO. OF ROOMS	6 w/shared baths 2 penthouses w/private baths
RATES	Rooms/Sgl/61.60 Dbl/$72.80 Penthouses/$140 Reservation/cancellation policy
CREDIT CARDS	American Express, Discover, MasterCard, Visa
BREAKFAST	Full, served in dining room or parlor Lunch & dinner available in restaurant Candlelight dinners in parlor available
AMENITIES	TV/radio & air conditioning in all rooms; jacuzzis in penthouses, fireplace & kitchen w/skylight in 1; complementary draft beer or wine on arrival
RESTRICTIONS	No pets
REVIEWED	*Bed & Breakfast: Southern California*

LEMON COVE

On the high road into Giant Forest Village of Sequoia National Park and very handy to fishing in Lake Kewah. The location doesn't get any better than this, about 14 miles east of Visalia on Hwy. 198.

LEMON COVE BED & BREAKFAST

33038 Sierra Dr.   Lemon Cove, CA 93244   (209) 597-2555
Patrick & Kay Bonette, Resident Owners

LOCATION	Exit Hwy. 198 at Hwy. 99, continue through town, on right
OPEN	All Year
DESCRIPTION	1968 2-story California Monterey English Country furnishings
NO. OF ROOMS	7 w/private baths 2 w/shared bath
RATES	PB/$65-89 SB/$55-59 Reservation/cancellation policy
CREDIT CARDS	American Express, Discover, MasterCard, Visa
BREAKFAST	Full, served in dining room
AMENITIES	Courtyard w/gazebo, full veranda & large deck; all rooms w/queen or king beds & fireplaces, whirlpool tub in 1 room, TV/radio in some rooms; complimentary refreshments; small meeting facilities
RESTRICTIONS	No smoking. No pets (resident dog & cats)
REVIEWED	*America's Wonderful Little Hotels & Inns* *Bed & Breakfast in California* *Bed & Breakfast: Southern California* *Complete Guide to Bed & Breakfasts, Inns & Guesthouses*
RSO	Eye Openers B&B Reservations

LONG BEACH

Once the Coney Island of the west, now California's fifth largest city and a tourist hot-spot. Head for Pier 1 and Howard Hughes' Spruce Goose, board the Queen Mary or trip around Londontowne. Cruises to Catalina leave frequently or head for Cabrillo Beach and Point Fermin Marine Life Refuge. the Toyota Grand Prix in April is world-class auto racing. But do spend a day in Naples, a little jewel of three islands separated by canals and linked by walkways. Hop a gondola for a little Italian experience. On the ocean, at the southern end of Los Angeles County, via three major highways.

LORD MAYOR'S INN BED & BREAKFAST

435 Cedar Ave.   Long Beach, CA 90802   *(310) 436-0324*
Laura & Reuben Brasser, Resident Owners

LOCATION	Exit Hwy. 710 at 6th St., proceed to 2nd traffic light, right on Cedar for 1/2 block
OPEN	All Year
DESCRIPTION	1904 2-story Classic Edwardian Turn-of-Century furnishings Long Beach Historic Register
NO. OF ROOMS	5 w/private baths
RATES	$65-95 Reservation/cancellation policy
CREDIT CARDS	American Express, MasterCard, Visa
BREAKFAST	Full, served in dining room or on porch
AMENITIES	Full rear deck, 2 front porches, 3 common areas; phone in rooms; complimentary evening refreshments
RESTRICTIONS	No smoking
AWARDS	National Trust 1992 Great American Home Award
REVIEWED	*American Historic Bed & Breakfast Inns & Guesthouses* *Bed & Breakfast: Southern California*
MEMBER	Bed & Breakfast Inns of Southern California
RATED	AAA 2 Diamonds

LOS ALAMOS
(SOLVANG)

About 15 miles south of Santa Maria on Hwy. 101. Near Vandenberg Air Force Base. In the heart of the flourishing Santa Ynez Valley wine country you will find wine tasting, antiquing, missions and the Danish village of Solvang.

THE UNION HOTEL

362 Bell St.   PO Box 616   Los Alamos, CA 93440   *(805) 344-2744*
Dick Langdon, Manager   *FAX: (805) 344-3125*

LOCATION	Center of town
OPEN	All Year (Friday-Sunday only)
DESCRIPTION	1880 Wells Fargo Stage Coach Stop with restaurant & full bar saloon Antique furnishings
NO. OF ROOMS	2 w/private baths 11 w/shared baths
RATES	PB/$110 SB/$90
	Reservation/cancellation policy
CREDIT CARDS	American Express, MasterCard, Visa
BREAKFAST	Full, served in dining room Dinner available in restaurant
AMENITIES	Park-like grounds w/swimming pool & jacuzzi; library; ping-pong room; pool room; shuffleboard in saloon; complimentary rides in a 1918 White touring car (if it's running)
RESTRICTIONS	No pets (resident cat). No children
REVIEWED	*American Historic Bed & Breakfast Inns & Guesthouses* *Bed & Breakfast in California* *Bed & Breakfast: Southern California* *Best Places to Stay in California* *Complete Guide to Bed & Breakfasts, Inns & Guesthouses* *Fodor's Bed & Breakfasts, Country Inns & Other Weekend Pleasures— The West Coast*

THE VICTORIAN MANSION

362 Bell St.   PO Box 616   Los Alamos, CA 93440
Dick Langdon, Owner

(805) 344-2744
FAX: (805) 344-2744

LOCATION	Center of town, adjacent to Union Hotel
OPEN	All Year
DESCRIPTION	1864 2-story Victorian Fantasy theme rooms
NO. OF ROOMS	6 w/private baths
RATES	$220 Reservation/cancellation policy
CREDIT CARDS	American Express, MasterCard, Visa
BREAKFAST	Full, delivered to room Dinner available in Union Hotel Friday-Sunday
AMENITIES	Swimming pool; private hot tubs, costume robes, fireplaces, TV/radio, phones, classic movies & background music in rooms; complimentary fruit, crackers, champagne or sparkling cider
RESTRICTIONS	No pets (resident cat). No children
REVIEWED	*American Historic Bed & Breakfast Inns & Guesthouses* *Bed & Breakfast: Southern California* *Best Places to Stay in California* *Complete Guide to Bed & Breakfasts, Inns & Guesthouses* *Fodor's Bed & Breakfasts, Country Inns & Other Weekend Pleasures—* *The West Coast*

LOS ANGELES

The state's largest city is second-largest in the nation. In the sprawling behemoth known as Greater Los Angeles, there really is a downtown L.A. Within and around its impressive and vital Civic Center are three major art museums, the tri-theater Music Center for the Performing Arts, Natural History Museum, a sunken shopping mall, El Pueblo de los Angeles Historical Monument and the mini-nations of Chinatown, Little Tokyo and Olvera Street.

THE CSOSCHKE'S

(RSO)   *Reservations: (415) 696-1690   FAX: (415) 696-1699*

LOCATION	In Century City
OPEN	All Year
DESCRIPTION	1950s Ranch Eclectic furnishings
NO. OF ROOMS	1 w/private bath
RATES	$60-68 Reservation/cancellation policy 2-night minimum stay
CREDIT CARDS	MasterCard, Visa
BREAKFAST	Continental plus, served in dining room overlooking garden
AMENITIES	TV/radio in rooms; handicapped access
RESTRICTIONS	No smoking. No pets
RSO	B&B International

Fairway House

(RSO)   *Reservations: (415) 696-1690   FAX: (415) 696-1699*

LOCATION	In Woodland Hills
OPEN	All Year
DESCRIPTION	1930s 2-story Spanish Mansion Antique furnishings
NO. OF ROOMS	6 w/private baths
RATES	$85-125 Reservation/cancellation policy 2-night minimum stay
CREDIT CARDS	MasterCard, Visa
BREAKFAST	Continental plus, served in dining room
AMENITIES	TV/radio & phones in rooms; handicapped access
RESTRICTIONS	No smoking. No pets
RSO	B&B International

Ginther's Bed & Breakfast

(RSO)   *Reservations: (415) 696-1690   FAX: (415) 696-1699*

LOCATION	In Westwood, near UCLA
OPEN	All Year
DESCRIPTION	1960s Contemporary Apartment Building Contemporary furnishings
NO. OF ROOMS	2 w/private baths
RATES	$70 Reservation/cancellation policy 2-night minimum stay
CREDIT CARDS	MasterCard, Visa
BREAKFAST	Continental plus, served in dining room
AMENITIES	TV/radio in rooms
RESTRICTIONS	No smoking. No pets (resident outdoor dogs)
RSO	B&B International

THE INN AT 657

657 W. 23rd St.   Los Angeles, CA 90007   (213) 741-2200
Patsy H. Carter, Resident Owner   (800) 347-7512

LOCATION	Downtown, 1 block west of Figueroa St. (main north/south street), across from the downtown campus of Mount St. Mary's College
OPEN	All Year
DESCRIPTION	1940 restored 2-story Tudor Apartment House Eclectic furnishings
NO. OF ROOMS	5 suites w/private baths
RATES	$95 Reservation/cancellation policy
CREDIT CARDS	No
BREAKFAST	Full, served in main dining room Special meals available
AMENITIES	Garden hot tub, sauna; all rooms w/cable TV/VCR/radios, goose down comforters, fresh flowers, some w/fully equipped kitchens, 1 w/private balcony & garden bath; video tape library; small meeting facilities; complimentary beverages, fresh fruit & snacks
RESTRICTIONS	No smoking. No pets
REVIEWED	*America's Wonderful Little Hotels & Inns* *Bed & Breakfast: Southern California*

SALISBURY HOUSE

2273 W. 20th St.   Los Angeles, CA 90018   (213) 737-7817
Sue & Jay German, Resident Owners   (800) 373-1778

LOCATION	In West Adams Historic District. From Santa Monica Freeway 10, go north on Western Ave., then take 1st left on 20th St.
OPEN	All Year
DESCRIPTION	1909 3-story California Craftsman Craftsman furnishings
NO. OF ROOMS	3 w/private baths 2 w/shared bath
RATES	PB/$80-100 SB/$65-75 Reservation/cancellation policy
CREDIT CARDS	American Express, Discover, MasterCard, Visa
BREAKFAST	Full, served in dining room
AMENITIES	Down comforters & pillows; robes; TV/radio in rooms; complimentary afternoon beverages & shortbread; facilities for small meetings & special events
RESTRICTIONS	No smoking. No pets
REVIEWED	*American Historic Bed & Breakfast Inns & Guesthouses* *Bed & Breakfast Homes Directory: West Coast* *Bed & Breakfast in California* *Bed & Breakfast: Southern California* *California Country Inns & Itineraries* *Complete Guide to Bed & Breakfasts, Inns & Guesthouses* *Country Inns & Back Roads: California* *The National Trust Guide to Historic Bed & Breakfasts, Inns & Small Hotels*
MEMBER	B&B Innkeepers of Southern California
RATED	AAA 2 Diamonds Mobil 2 Stars

THE SCHOENY'S

Reservations: (415) 696-1690   *FAX: (415) 696-1699*

LOCATION	In The Silverlake District off of Sunset
OPEN	All Year
DESCRIPTION	1950s 2-Story Ranch Eclectic furnishings
NO. OF ROOMS	1 apartment w/private bath
RATES	$65 Reservation/cancellation policy 2-night minimum stay
CREDIT CARDS	MasterCard, Visa
BREAKFAST	Continental, provided in apartment
AMENITIES	TV/radio & phone in apartment
RESTRICTIONS	No smoking. No pets
RSO	B&B International

LOS OLIVOS

The excellent wineries here are a good reason to visit. Tours and tastings are available at the huge Firestone Vineyard and the Zaca Mesa Winery. The town's restored buildings are an attaction, too. Northwest of Santa Barbara via Hwys. 101 and 154.

LOS OLIVOS GRAND HOTEL

2860 Grand Ave.   PO Box 526   Los Olivos, CA 93441   *(805) 688-7788*
Michael Healey, Manager   *(800) 446-2455   FAX: (805) 688-1942*

LOCATION	From Hwy. 101 take Hwy. 154 approx. 2 mi. to Grand Ave., turn left if coming from the north, or right if from the south. Hotel is just past flagpole, check-in on left
OPEN	All Year
DESCRIPTION	1986 2-story Victorian Country Inn w/Restaurant French Country furnishings
NO. OF ROOMS	21 w/private baths
RATES	Weekends/$210-325 Weekdays/$160-300 Reservation/cancellation policy 2-night minimum stay on weekends
CREDIT CARDS	Diner's Club, MasterCard, Visa
BREAKFAST	Continental, served in guest rooms Dinner & lunch available in restaurant
AMENITIES	Patio, arbor & gazebo, swimming pool, jacuzzi; fireplace, TV/radio, phones, wet bar, complimentary wine & refrigerator in rooms; down comforters; conference room & meeting facilities; handicapped access
RESTRICTIONS	No pets
REVIEWED	*California Country Inns & Itineraries* *Complete Guide to Bed & Breakfasts, Inns & Guesthouses*
RATED	AAA 4 Diamonds Mobil 4 Stars

Los Osos

Originally named La Cañada de los Osos, "Valley of the Bears." Gateway to Montana de Oro State Park, one of the state's most beautiful, halfway between San Luis Obispo and Morro Bay on Hwy. 101. Celebrate the Festival of the Bear at the end of August and Oktoberfest in October.

Gerarda's Bed & Breakfast

1056 Bay Oaks Dr.   Los Osos, CA 93402   *(805) 528-3973*
Gerarda Ondang, Resident Owner

LOCATION	In residential neighborhood
OPEN	All Year
DESCRIPTION	1961 Ranch Style Dutch furnishings
NO. OF ROOMS	2 w/private baths 1 w/shared bath
RATES	$30-45 Reservation/cancellation policy
CREDIT CARDS	No
BREAKFAST	Continental plus, served in Dutch kitchen
AMENITIES	TV in rooms; complimentary afternoon tea; small meeting facilities; handicapped access
RESTRICTIONS	No smoking. No pets (resident dogs & cat)
REVIEWED	*Affordable Bed & Breakfasts* *Bed & Breakfast U.S.A.* *Complete Guide to Bed & Breakfasts, Inns & Guesthouses*
RSO	B&B of Los Angeles Eye Openers B&B Reservations

Homestays

(RSO)   *Reservations: (805) 544-4406   FAX: (805) 546-8642*

There are three homestays available in Los Osos from Megan's Friends B&B Reservation Service.

MALIBU

There's dramatic beauty in the winding, mountainous canyons and some splendid beaches where surfing, body-watching and beachcombing for celebrities are local culture. Don't miss Malibu Lagoon State Park, a haven for native and migratory birds; or the grounds and collections of J. Paul Getty Museum. On Pacific Coast Highway north of Santa Monica.

CASA LARRONDE

PO Box 86 Malibu, CA 90265   *(310) 456-9333*
Charlou Larronde, Resident Owner

LOCATION	On the beach known as Millionaire's Row, 12 mi. north of Santa Monica, 1 mi. south of Mailbu Pier
OPEN	October-July
DESCRIPTION	1951 2-story elegant Contemporary Eclectic furnishings
NO. OF ROOMS	2 w/private baths
RATES	Guestroom/$100 Ocean Suite/$115 Reservation/cancellation policy
CREDIT CARDS	No
BREAKFAST	Full, served in dining area overlooking ocean, or on ocean deck
AMENITIES	Suite has fireplace, sitting area, floor-to-ceiling ocean-view windows, private deck & mini kitchen; TV/radio, phone in rooms; complimentary champagne, cocktails & hors d'oeuvres; small meeting facilities, handicapped access
RESTRICTIONS	No smoking. No pets. Inquire about children
REVIEWED	*Bed & Breakfast in California* *Bed & Breakfast U.S.A.*

MALIBU BEACH INN

22878 *Pacific Coast Hwy.*   *Malibu, CA 90265*   *(800) 462-5428*
Dan Ferrante, Manager   *(310) 456-6444*
Marty & Vicki Cooper and Skip & Lee Miser, Owners   FAX: *(310) 456-1499*

LOCATION	On the beach at Malibu Pier, 12 mi. north of Santa Monica
OPEN	All Year
DESCRIPTION	1989 3-story Mission Style Hotel Southwestern & contemporary furnishings
NO. OF ROOMS	47 w/private baths
RATES	$115-290 Inquire about special "Beach Club Service" package Reservation/cancellation policy 2-night minimum stay
CREDIT CARDS	American Express, Diner's Club, MasterCard, Visa
BREAKFAST	California Continental plus, served on patio overlooking ocean (From Alice's Restaurant)
AMENITIES	All rooms w/private ocean front balconies, TV/VCR/radio, phone, wet bar & safe, most w/fireplaces; videos available, small meeting facilities; limited handicapped access
RESTRICTIONS	No pets. Inquire about children
RATED	AAA 3 Diamonds

MALIBU COUNTRY INN

6506 *Westward Beach Rd. Malibu, CA 90265*
Larry Keating, Manager

(310) 457-9622
FAX: (310) 457-1349

LOCATION	North on Pacific Coast Hwy. to Westward Beach Rd. (before Zuma Beach)
OPEN	All Year
DESCRIPTION	1940's renovated French Country Country furnishings On 3-acre garden site
NO. OF ROOMS	16 w/private baths
RATES	$95-225 Reservation/cancellation policy
CREDIT CARDS	American Express, MasterCard, Visa
BREAKFAST	Full, served in breakfast room by the pool
AMENITIES	Heated swimming pool & sun deck; all rooms w/TV/radio, phones, refrigerator, coffeemaker, fruit basket & fresh flowers, most w/private patios; small meeting facilities; handicapped access
RESTRICTIONS	No smoking. Inquire about pets. No children
RATED	AAA 2 Diamonds

Marina Del Rey
(Santa Monica)

This is true: here is the largest man-made boat harbor in the world, a good place to soak up the yatchy ambiance. Cruise the harbor on a Mississippi riverboat (really) and sample the upscale goodies at Cape Cod-style Fisherman's Village.

The Mansion Inn

327 Washington Blvd.   Marina Del Rey, CA 90291   *(310) 821-2557*
Richard Hunnicutt, Manager   *(800) 828-0688   FAX: (310) 827-0289*

LOCATION	1 block from Venice Beach. Exit Hwy. 405 South to Freeway 90, right on Lincoln, left on Washington Blvd., 1 mi. on right. Around the corner from the Venice Strand
OPEN	All Year
DESCRIPTION	1977 4-story Mediterranean Inn French Country furnishings
NO. OF ROOMS	38 w/private baths 5 2-level suites w/private baths & living rooms
RATES	$69-125 Reservation/cancellation policy
CREDIT CARDS	All major credit cards
BREAKFAST	Continental plus, served in courtyard or Courtyard Cafe
AMENITIES	TV/radio, phones, stocked refrigerator, hair dryers in rooms; handicapped access; complimentary off-street parking, morning newspaper
RESTRICTIONS	No pets
REVIEWED	*Bed & Breakfast Inns* *California Dream Days* *Inn Places for Bed & Breakfast*
RATED	AAA 3 Diamonds

MARINA BED & BREAKFAST

PO Box 11828   Marina Del Rey, CA 90295   *(310) 821-9862*
Carolyn & Peter Griswold, Resident Owners

LOCATION	Freeway 405 to Freeway 90 West to end. Right on Lincoln, left on Washington, left on Oxford
OPEN	All Year
DESCRIPTION	1989 Contemporary Contemporary furnishings
NO. OF ROOMS	1 w/private bath
RATES	$55-60 Reservation/cancellation policy 2-night minimum stay
CREDIT CARDS	No
BREAKFAST	Continental plus, served in guestroom
AMENITIES	TV/radio in room; roof-top deck; bicycles available
RESTRICTIONS	No smoking. No pets (resident dog). Children over 12
REVIEWED	*Bed & Breakfast Homes Directory: West Coast* *Bed & Breakfast U.S.A.* *Complete Guide to Bed & Breakfasts, Inns & Guesthouses*
RSO	B&B of Los Angeles

MONTEREY
(MONTEREY PENINSULA)

Approaching this scenic wonder via the 17-Mile Drive overloads the senses: seascapes fit for Heathcliffe, enchanted forests of pines and gnarled cypress, world-class golf courses (Pebble Beach) and palatial estates. But watch where you step; there are "no trespassing" signs everywhere. The town offers up historic Cannery Row, Fisherman's Wharf, Customs House Plaza and the incredible Monterey Bay Aquarium's undersea habitats. The undersea canyon in this region is larger and deeper than the Grand Canyon. The list goes on. You just have to be here.

DEL MONTE BEACH INN

1110 Del Monte Ave.   Monterey, CA 93940
Lisa Glover, Manager

(408) 649-4411
FAX: (408) 372-9632

LOCATION	1/2 mi. from Fisherman's Wharf, across the street from the beach
OPEN	All Year
DESCRIPTION	1919 3-story European Pensione Turn-of-century furnishings
NO. OF ROOMS	2 w/private baths 16 w/shared baths
RATES	PB/$75-80 SB/$55-75 Reservation/cancellation policy
CREDIT CARDS	Discover, MasterCard, Visa
BREAKFAST	Continental plus buffet, served in parlor
AMENITIES	Fresh flowers & comforters in rooms, most w/queen size beds; complimentary beverages & cookies; wedding/meeting facilities
RESTRICTIONS	No smoking. No pets
REVIEWED	*American Historic Bed & Breakfast Inns & Guesthouses* *Bed & Breakfast in California* *Complete Guide to Bed & Breakfasts, Inns & Guesthouses*

THE JABBERWOCK INN

598 Laine St.   Monterey, CA 93940   *(408) 372-4777*
Barbara & Jim Allen, Resident Owners

LOCATION	4 blocks above Cannery Row & Monterey Bay Aquarium, on corner of Laine & Hoffman
OPEN	All Year
DESCRIPTION	1911 2-story post-Victorian Eclectic furnishings
NO. OF ROOMS	3 w/private baths 4 w/shared baths
RATES	PB/$145-175 SB/$100-120 Reservation/cancellation policy 2-night minimum stay on weekends
CREDIT CARDS	MasterCard, Visa
BREAKFAST	Full, served in dining room, sunporch or guestroom
AMENITIES	Enclosed veranda, half-acre gardens w/waterfalls; robes, down comforters & pillows, fresh flowers, fireplace & radio in rooms; phone available; complimentary sherry & hors d'oeuvres, juices & soda, & bedtime milk & cookies; small meeting facilities; private parking
RESTRICTIONS	No smoking. No pets (resident English Bull Terriers)
REVIEWED	*American Historic Bed & Breakfast Inns & Guesthouses* *America's Wonderful Little Hotels & Inns* *Bed & Breakfast American Style* *Bed & Breakfast in California* *Best Places to Stay in California* *Complete Guide to Bed & Breakfasts, Inns & Guesthouses* *Country Inns & Back Roads: California* *Country Inns of the Far West: California* *Fodor's Bed & Breakfasts, Country Inns & Other Weekend Pleasures—* *The West Coast*
MEMBER	California Assn. of B&B Inns Professional Assn. of Innkeepers International
RATED	Mobil 3 Stars

MERRITT HOUSE

386 Pacific St.   Monterey, CA 93940   (408) 646-9686   (800) 541-5599
Jeffrey Hirsch, Manager   FAX: (408) 646-5392

LOCATION	Exit Hwy. 1 at Delmonte, left on Pacific (downtown), first driveway on right
OPEN	All Year
DESCRIPTION	1830 2-story Adobe w/1978 addition Antique furnishings National Historic Register
NO. OF ROOMS	25 w/private baths
RATES	Balcony & Terrace Rooms/$99-130 Suites/$175-195 Reservation/cancellation policy Inquire about group rates
CREDIT CARDS	Diner's Club, Discover, MasterCard, Visa
BREAKFAST	Continental plus, served in common room
AMENITIES	All rooms have king or queen beds, fireplaces, TV/radio & phones; small meeting facilities; handicapped access, off-street parking
RESTRICTIONS	Smoking limited. No pets
REVIEWED	*American Historic Bed & Breakfast Inns & Guesthouses* *Complete Guide to Bed & Breakfasts, Inns & Guesthouses*
RATED	AAA 3 Diamonds Mobil 3 Stars

THE MONTEREY HOTEL

406 Alvarado St.   Monterey, CA 93940
Edith McGee, Manager

(408) 375-3184
FAX: (408) 373-2899

LOCATION	From Freemont turn right Alvarado
OPEN	All Year
DESCRIPTION	1904 2-story European Inn Eclectic furnishings
NO. OF ROOMS	44 w/private baths
RATES	$85 Reservation/cancellation policy
CREDIT CARDS	American Express, Discover, MasterCard, Visa
BREAKFAST	Continental plus, served in dining room
AMENITIES	TV/radio & phone in rooms, some w/fireplaces; complimentary tea, & evening milk & cookies; meeting facilities
RESTRICTIONS	No pets (resident dog)
REVIEWED	*American Historic Bed & Breakfast Inns & Guesthouses* *Complete Guide to Bed & Breakfasts, Inns & Guesthouses*
RATED	Mobil 2 Stars

OLD MONTEREY INN

500 Martin St.   Monterey, CA 93940   *(408) 375-8284   (800) 350-2344*
Ann & Gene Swett, Resident Owners

LOCATION	From Hwy. 1 South, take Soledad/Munras exit, cross Munras Ave., right on Pacific St., 1/2 mi. to Martin St., on left
	From Hwy. 1 North, take Munras Ave. Exit, immediate left on Soledad Dr., right on Pacific St., 1/2 mi. to Martin St., on left
OPEN	All Year
DESCRIPTION	1920's 3-story English Tudor Antique & period furnishings
NO. OF ROOMS	10 w/private baths Includes Garden cottage & suite
RATES	$160-220 Reservation/cancellation policy 2-night minimum on weekends
CREDIT CARDS	MasterCard, Visa
BREAKFAST	Full, served in dining room, in guestrooms on tray, or in bed
AMENITIES	Landscaped gardens; all rooms have robes, down comforters & pillows, & sitting area, most have fireplaces, skylights & stained glass windows; radios & phones available; complimentary afternoon tea & evening wine & hors d'oeuvres
RESTRICTIONS	No smoking. No pets (resident German Shepherd)
AWARDS	The Best of 1991, *Country Inns Magazine* Inn of the Year 1992, *Focus Magazine*
REVIEWED	*American Historic Bed & Breakfast Inns & Guesthouses* *America's Wonderful Little Hotels & Inns* *Bed & Breakfast in California* *Best Places to Stay in California* *Complete Guide to Bed & Breakfasts, Inns & Guesthouses* *Country Inns & Back Roads: California* *Fodor's Bed & Breakfasts, Country Inns & Other Weekend Pleasures—* *The West Coast*
MEMBER	California Assn. of B&B Inns Professional Assn. of Innkeepers International
RATED	Mobil 4 Stars

MORRO BAY

That great 576-foot volcanic monolith jutting from the Bay is a protected nesting site for endangereed Peregrine Falcons. Extending four miles toward the Rock is the sandspit, an area teeming with sand dunes and sea life that's accessible by shuttle boat. Good times to be here include the Morro Bay Triathlon near the end of September, and the town celebrates its Harbor Boat Parade in very early December. But don't miss the Morro Bay State Park. The coastal ribbon of Hwy. 101 ends here, about 15 miles northwets of San Luis Obispo.

COFFEY BREAK BED & BREAKFAST

213 Dunes Street   Morro Bay, CA 93442   *(805) 772-4378*
Don & Roberta Coffey, Resident Owners

LOCATION	1 block to Bay. Exit Hwy. 1 at Morro Bay Blvd., west to Market Ave., right to Dunes St., left to house.
OPEN	All Year
DESCRIPTION	1989 Frame Home
NO. OF ROOMS	3 w/private baths
RATES	$75-$85
CREDIT CARDS	No
BREAKFAST	Continental plus, served in dining room
AMENITIES	Ocean and bay views; queen beds; TV in rooms; private entrances
RESTRICTIONS	No smoking. No pets. No children.

HOMESTAY

RSO   *Reservations: (805) 544-4406   FAX: (805) 546-8642*

LOCATION	Near golf course
OPEN	All Year
DESCRIPTION	Custom-built Contemporary Home Eclectic furnishings
NO. OF ROOMS	2 w/private baths 1 w/shared bath (Including 1 suite)
RATES	$75 Reservation/cancellation policy
CREDIT CARDS	No
BREAKFAST	Rooms/Full, served in family room Suite/Continental, provided in suite
AMENITIES	Fireplaces & TV/radios in family room & den
RESTRICTIONS	No smoking. No pets (resident outside cat). Children okay in suite.
RSO	Megan's Friends B&B Reservation Service

NEWPORT BEACH
(ORANGE CO.)

This melange of man-made islands is a kind of summer place and bastion of Orange County's high society. This is a place where boats outnumber cars — 10,000 bob around in Newport Harbor — and yatch clubs proliferate. In June, the annual Flight of the Snowbirds Regatta is a major event. Other things worth visiting include the Newport Harbor Art Museum and the Upper Newport Bay Ecological Reserve, southern California's largest estuary, is a vital stopover for migrating birds on the Pacific flyway. On the Pacific Coast Highway, south of Long Beach.

BAY SHORES INN

1800 W. Balboa Blvd. Newport Beach, CA 92663
Bill Pratt, Manager

(800) 222-6675
FAX: (714) 675-4977

LOCATION	On the beach at 18th St. & Balboa Blvd. (Newport Blvd. becomes Balboa)
OPEN	All Year
DESCRIPTION	1970 Inn Eclectic furnishings
NO. OF ROOMS	20 w/private baths 2-bedroom suite w/full kitchen & private bath
RATES	Sgl/$85-99 Dbl/$92-109 Suite/$170-219 Reservation/cancellation policy Inquire about corporate rates
CREDIT CARDS	All major cards
BREAKFAST	Continental, served in breakfast room
AMENITIES	Sundeck on roof; king & queen beds, TV/VCR & phones in rooms; playground & children's activities; library; use of beach chairs & sports equipment; bicycle rental service; FAX; complimentary morning paper, afternoon fruit & tea, & video library; laundry facilities, beach parking
RESTRICTIONS	No pets
RATED	AAA 3 Diamonds Mobil 2 Stars

DORYMAN'S OCEANFRONT INN BED & BREAKFAST

2102 W. OceanFront   Newport Beach, CA 92663   (714) 675-7300
Michael & Laura Palitz, Resident Owners

LOCATION	Hwy. 55 South to Newport Beach Pier. On right side of pier
OPEN	All Year
DESCRIPTION	1891 2-story Victorian Victorian & French Country furnishings National Historic Register
NO. OF ROOMS	10 w/private baths
RATES	$135-275 Reservation/cancellation policy
CREDIT CARDS	American Express, Diner's Club, MasterCard, Visa
BREAKFAST	Full or continental, served in parlour, oceanfront patio, or in bed
AMENITIES	Robes; fireplaces, down comforters, sunken bath tubs, TV/radio, phone in rooms; complimentary refreshments; meeting facilities; handicapped access
RESTRICTIONS	None
REVIEWED	*American Historic Bed & Breakfast Inns & Guesthouses* *America's Wonderful Little Hotels & Inns* *Bed & Breakfast in California* *Bed & Breakfast: Southern California* *Best Places to Stay in California* *California Country Inns & Itineraries* *Complete Guide to Bed & Breakfasts, Inns & Guesthouses*
MEMBER	California Hotel /Motel Assn.
RSO	California Riviera 800

THE LITTLE INN ON THE BAY

617 Lido Park Dr.   Newport Beach, CA 92663   *(714) 673-8800*
Laura Ann Laing, Manager   *(800) 438-4466*

LOCATION	On the right side of Newport Pier
OPEN	All Year
DESCRIPTION	1961 Country Cape Cod furnishings
NO. OF ROOMS	29 w/private baths
RATES	$100 Reservation/cancellation policy
CREDIT CARDS	American Express, MasterCard, Visa
BREAKFAST	Continental, served in breakfast area Dinner & lunch available
AMENITIES	Swimming pool; TV/radio & phone in rooms; complimentary wine & cheese, cookies, milk & hot chocolate; meeting facilities
RESTRICTIONS	No smoking. No pets
REVIEWED	*America's Wonderful Little Hotels & Inns* *Complete Guide to Bed & Breakfasts, Inns & Guesthouses*
RATED	AAA 3 Diamonds

NIPOMO

Citrus orchards, vegetable farms, commercial nurseries, eucalyptus trees and vineyards cover the landscape. Taste the grapes at Ross-Keller Wineries. On a scenic stretch of Hwy. 101, 16 miles south of San Luis Obispo.

THE KALEIDOSCOPE INN

130 E. Dana St.   PO Box 1297   Nipomo, CA 93444   *(805) 929-5444*
Pat & Bill Linane, Resident Owners

LOCATION	Exit Hwy. 101 at Tefft, east to Thompson Rd., right 1 block, left on Dana St.
OPEN	All Year
DESCRIPTION	1886 2-story Gingerbread Victorian Antique Victorian furnishings
NO. OF ROOMS	3 w/private baths
RATES	$75-80 Reservation/cancellation policy
CREDIT CARDS	American Express, MasterCard, Visa
BREAKFAST	Full, served in dining room, garden or guestrooms
AMENITIES	Queen beds, robes, jacuzzi tubs; TV/radio in library; complimentary refreshments; garden w/gazebo; meeting/wedding facilities
RESTRICTIONS	No smoking. No pets (resident cats & dog)
AWARDS	1992 Home Beautiful Award, Nipomo Chamber of Commerce
REVIEWED	*American Historic Bed & Breakfast Inns & Guesthouses* *America's Wonderful Little Hotels & Inns* *Bed & Breakfast: Southern California* *Best Bed & Breakfasts & Country Inns: West* *The Painted Ladies Guide to Victorian California*

NIPTON

The northeast access point into the East Mojave National Scenic Area, America's first such designated area. Get good information and directions before venturing into the interior. About 10 miles from the Nevada border via I-15.

HOTEL NIPTON

72 Nipton Rd. HC1, Box 357   Nipton, CA 92364   *(619) 856-2335*
Gerald & Roxanne Freeman, Owners

LOCATION	10 mi. east of I-15 Nipton Rd. Exit
OPEN	All Year
DESCRIPTION	1904 Hotel Southwestern Antique furnishings
NO. OF ROOMS	4 share 2 baths
RATES	$45 Reservation/cancellation policy
CREDIT CARDS	Diner's Club, MasterCard, Visa
BREAKFAST	Continental, served in parlor
AMENITIES	Outdoor hot tub
RESTRICTIONS	No pets
REVIEWED	*American Historic Bed & Breakfast Inns & Guesthouses* *America's Wonderful Little Hotels & Inns* *Bed & Breakfast in California* *Bed & Breakfast: Southern California* *Bed & Breakfast U.S.A.* *Complete Guide to Bed & Breakfasts, Inns & Guesthouses*

OJAI

The extraordinary location of this idyllic, wealthy Shangri-La has made it a significant artist's colony and magnet for mystics. The 118-acre estate of the Krotona Institute of Theosophy is open to visitors, as is the Krishnamurti Foundation. The Ojai Music Festival is June is a major event. Soak in the spas at Matilija Hot Springs and Wheeler Hot Springs. Lake Casitas is a treasure-trove of coves and inlets. At the edge of the Los Padres National Forest, 15 miles inland from Ventura via Hwy. 33.

BUSHMAN'S BED & BREAKFAST

1220 N. Montgomery St.   Ojai, CA 93023   *(805) 646-4295*
Pat Bushman, Resident Owner

LOCATION	From Ojai Ave., north on Montgomery St., then detour by turning right on Grand, left on Daly, and left on Andrew St. to arrive back at Montgomery. House is last one on right
OPEN	All Year
DESCRIPTION	1967 California Spanish Contemporary (casual) furnishings
NO. OF ROOMS	4 share 1-1/2 baths
RATES	$65 Reservation/cancellation policy
CREDIT CARDS	No
BREAKFAST	Full, served in dining room
AMENITIES	Complimentary tea & coffee
RESTRICTIONS	No smoking. No pets. No children
REVIEWED	*Bed & Breakfast in California*
RSO	B&B of Los Angeles

CASA DE LA LUNA BED & BREAKFAST

710 S. La Luna Ave.   Ojai, CA 93023   (805) 646-4528
Doris Scott, Resident Owner

LOCATION	From Hwy. 150 north, left on 2nd St., north on La Luna
OPEN	All Year
DESCRIPTION	1978 Mexican Hacienda Antique furnishings
NO. OF ROOMS	7 w/private baths
RATES	$80-95 Reservation/cancellation policy
CREDIT CARDS	No
BREAKFAST	Full gourmet, served in formal dining room
AMENITIES	Exotic formal gardens & fine arts gallery; handicapped access
RESTRICTIONS	No smoking. No pets. Children 12 & over
MEMBER	Ojai Valley Chamber of Commerce Innkeepers

OJAI MANOR HOTEL

210 E. Matilija   Ojai, CA 93023   (805) 646-0961
Mary Nelson, Resident Owner

LOCATION	Downtown, 1 block north of Hwy. 150
OPEN	All Year
DESCRIPTION	1874 Western Eclectic furnishings
NO. OF ROOMS	6 share 3 baths
RATES	$80-90 Reservation/cancellation policy
CREDIT CARDS	MasterCard, Visa
BREAKFAST	Continental plus, served in dining room
AMENITIES	Complimentary wine & soft drinks; meeting facilities
RESTRICTIONS	No smoking. No children. Resident cats

THEODORE WOOLSEY HOUSE

1484 E. Ojai Ave.   Ojai, CA 93023   *(805) 646-9779*
Ana Cross, Resident Owner

LOCATION	1 mi. past stop light
OPEN	All Year
DESCRIPTION	1887 2-story Connecticut Farmhouse Antique & eclectic furnishings City of Ojai Historic Landmark
NO. OF ROOMS	3 w/private baths 3 w/shared baths
RATES	PB/$110 SB/$50-65 Reservation/cancellation policy 2-night minimum stay on weekends
CREDIT CARDS	No
BREAKFAST	Continental plus buffet, served in dining room
AMENITIES	Swimming pool & oversized deck; screened patio; piano & 1950's Juke box w/golden oldies in living room; fireplaces in 2 rooms, TV/radio in 3; complimentary refreshments
RESTRICTIONS	No smoking. No pets (resident cat). No children
REVIEWED	*Bed & Breakfast: Southern California* *Complete Guide to Bed & Breakfasts, Inns & Guesthouses*

ORANGE

The town's fruitful beginnings in 1869 sprouted from 1,300 acres given as payment to two lawyers. The town grew from around its circular Central Plaza. Wonderfully restored Victorian neighborhoods are worth a walking tour. Between Fullerton and Anaheim, and handy to the best of Orange County.

COUNTRY COMFORT BED & BREAKFAST

5104 E. Valencia Dr.   Orange, CA 92669   *(714) 532-2802*
Geri Lopker & Joanne Angell, Resident Owners

LOCATION	Exit Hwy. 55 at Katella, east 2 mi., pass Hewes, turn right on Linda Vista & right on Valencia
OPEN	All Year
DESCRIPTION	1960's glass & wood Eichler Country & antique furnishings
NO. OF ROOMS	2 w/private baths 1 w/shared bath
RATES	PB/$55-60 SB/$50-55 Reservation/cancellation policy 2-night minimum
CREDIT CARDS	No
BREAKFAST	Full, continental plus or continental, served in dining area
AMENITIES	Swimming pool, hot tub & patio; living room w/fireplace; cable TV/VCR in family room; King & Queen beds, TV/radio & phones in rooms; complimentary evening refreshments; bicycles; handicapped access
RESTRICTIONS	No smoking. No pets (resident 2-yr.-old Golden Retriever)
REVIEWED	*Bed & Breakfast U.S.A.*
MEMBER	B&B Innkeepers of Southern California

PACIFIC GROVE
(MONTEREY PENINSULA)

Now you know where the Monarch butterflies go: to Butterfly Trees Park, where they hang by the thousands in massive clusters resembling dried leaves from October to March. Other noteworthies include the still-operating 1885 Light House at Pt. Pinos Reserve, Pacific Grove Art Center, shopping at the American Tin Cannery, Asilomar State Beach, — and everything else in this area.

THE CENTRELLA

612 Central Ave.   Pacific Grove, CA 93950   (408) 372-3372
Joseph R. Megna, Co-General Partner   (800) 233-3372   FAX: (408) 372-2036

LOCATION	Where Holman Hwy. becomes Forest Ave., continue to Central Ave. & turn left for 2 blocks to corner of 17th St.
OPEN	All Year
DESCRIPTION	1898 2-story Victorian Victorian furnishings & Laura Ashley prints National Historic Register
NO. OF ROOMS	24 w/private baths 2 w/shared bath (Includes rooms, suites & cottages)
RATES	PB/$110-125 SB/$75-90 Reservation/cancellation policy 2-night minimum on weekends
CREDIT CARDS	American Express, MasterCard, Visa
BREAKFAST	Full buffet, served in dining/parlor area
AMENITIES	Robes; fireplace & TV/radio in some rooms; phone in rooms; complimentary evening wine & cheese; small meeting facilities; handicapped access; inquire about special packages
RESTRICTIONS	No smoking. No pets. Inquire about children
REVIEWED	*American Historic Bed & Breakfast Inns & Guesthouses* *America's Wonderful Little Hotels & Inns* *Bed & Breakfast in California* *Best Places to Stay in California* *Complete Guide to Bed & Breakfasts, Inns & Guesthouses*
RSO	Resort-II-Me
MEMBER	California Assn. of B&B Inns

GATEHOUSE INN BED & BREAKFAST

225 Central Ave.   Pacific Grove, CA 93950   *(800) 753-1881*
Kent & Joyce Cherry, Resident Owners   *FAX: (408) 648-8044*
Kristy Aslin, Manager

LOCATION	Hwy. 68 to Forest Ave., right on Central for 17 blocks to Inn
OPEN	All Year
DESCRIPTION	1884 2-story Italinate Victorian Victorian furnishings Full ocean views
NO. OF ROOMS	8 w/private baths
RATES	$95-170 Reservation/cancellation policy 2-night minimum stay on weekends
CREDIT CARDS	American Express, MasterCard, Visa
BREAKFAST	Full buffet, served in dining room
AMENITIES	Fireplaces in some rooms; queen beds, down comforters, radio & phones in all rooms; complimentary afternoon hors d'oeuvres, wine & tea; limited handicapped access
RESTRICTIONS	No smoking. No pets. Children over 12
REVIEWED	*American Historic Bed & Breakfast Inns & Guesthouses* *America's Wonderful Little Hotels & Inns* *Best Places to Kiss in Northern California* *Best Places to Stay in California* *Fodor's Bed & Breakfasts, Country Inns & Other Weekend Pleasures—* *The West Coas* *The National Trust Guide to Historic Bed & Breakfasts, Inns &* *Small Hotels*
MEMBER	American B&B Assn. California Assn. of B&B Inns National B&B Assn. Professional Assn. of Innkeepers International
RATED	ABBA A-

GOSBY HOUSE INN

643 Lighthouse Ave.   Pacific Grove, CA 93950   *(408) 375-1287*
Jillian Brewer, Manager   *FAX: (408) 655-9621*

LOCATION	From Hwy. 68, continue on Forest to Lighthouse, then left for 3 blocks
OPEN	All Year
DESCRIPTION	1887 2-story Queen Anne Victorian Antique & Country furnishings National Historic Register
NO. OF ROOMS	20 w/private baths 2 w/shared bath
RATES	PB/$85-135 SB/$100 Reservation/cancellation policy Inquire about corporate guest program
CREDIT CARDS	American Express, MasterCard, Visa
BREAKFAST	Full gourmet, served in dining room, or in guestroom for a small service charge
AMENITIES	Robes, fireplace, TV/radio & phone in rooms; evening turndown service; complimentary morning newspaper, beverages & afternoon tea & cookies; wine available; small meeting facilities
RESTRICTIONS	No smoking. No pets
REVIEWED	*American Historic Bed & Breakfast Inns & Guesthouses* *Bed & Breakfast: California: A Select Guide* *Bed & Breakfast in California* *Complete Guide to Bed & Breakfasts, Inns & Guesthouses*
MEMBER	California Assn. of B&B Inns
RATED	Mobil 2 Stars

GREEN GABLES INN

104 5th Street   Pacific Grove, CA 93950   *(408) 375-2095*
Shirley Butts, Manager

LOCATION	Take Forest (Hwy. 68) to Ocean, then right to 5th St.
OPEN	All Year
DESCRIPTION	1888 2-story Victorian Victorian Country furnishings National Historic Register
NO. OF ROOMS	7 w/private baths 4 w/shared baths
RATES	PB/$140-160 SB/$100-135 Reservation/cancellation policy
CREDIT CARDS	American Express, MasterCard, Visa
BREAKFAST	Full, served in dining room, or in guestroom for extra charge
AMENITIES	Robes, fireplace, TV/radio & phone in rooms; evening turndown service; complimentary morning newspaper, beverages & afternoon tea & cookies; wine available; small meeting facilities
RESTRICTIONS	No pets
REVIEWED	*American Historic Bed & Breakfast Inns & Guesthouses* *America's Wonderful Little Hotels & Inns* *Bed & Breakfast: California: A Select Guide* *Bed & Breakfast in California* *Best Places to Stay in California* *California Country Inns & Itineraries* *Complete Guide to Bed & Breakfasts, Inns & Guesthouses* *Country Inns & Back Roads: California* *Fodor's Bed & Breakfasts, Country Inns & Other Weekend Pleasures—* *The West Coast*
RATED	Mobil 3 Stars

THE MARTINE INN

255 Ocean View Blvd.   Pacific Grove, CA 93950   (408) 373-3388
Marion & Don Martine, Resident Owners   FAX: (408) 373-3896

LOCATION	From Forest Ave. (Hwy. 68), turn right on Ocean View Blvd. House is on right
OPEN	All Year
DESCRIPTION	1899 2-story Mediterranean Villa & Carriage House Authentic Victorian & American Antique furnishings
NO. OF ROOMS	19 w/private baths
RATES	$115-225 Reservation/cancellation policy 2-night minimum stay on weekends Inquire about minimum stay during holidays
CREDIT CARDS	MasterCard, Visa
BREAKFAST	Full, served in parlor overlooking Monterey Bay
AMENITIES	Spa room w/hot tub; courtyard w/pond & fountain; game room w/pool table & nickelodeon; complimentary evening wine & hors d'oeuvres, & morning newspaper; robes, phones, fresh fruit & flowers in all rooms, some w/fireplaces; off-street parking; small meeting facilities; handicapped access
RESTRICTIONS	Smoking limited. No pets
AWARDS	America's Top 12 B&Bs, *Country Inns Magazine*, Feb. 1992
REVIEWED	*America's Wonderful Little Hotels & Inns* *American Historic B&B Inns & Guesthouses* *Best Places to Stay in California* *Complete Guide to Bed & Breakfasts, Inns, & Guesthouses* *Fodor's Bed & Breakfasts, Country Inns, & Other Weekend Pleasures—The West Coast* *The National Trust Guide to Historic Bed & Breakfasts, Inns & Small Hotels*
MEMBER	California Assn. of Bed & Breakfast Inns

THE OLD ST. ANGELA INN

321 Central Ave.   Pacific Grove, CA 93950   *(408) 372-3246*
Don & Barbara Foster, Resident Owners   *FAX: (408) 375-3841*

LOCATION	From Monterey take Lighthouse to Pacific Grove, where it becomes Central Ave.
OPEN	All Year
DESCRIPTION	1910 2-story Cape Cod Antique pine furnishings
NO. OF ROOMS	6 w/private baths 3 w/shared baths
RATES	$90-150 Reservation/cancellation policy, 2-night minimum on weekends
CREDIT CARDS	American Express, MasterCard, Visa
BREAKFAST	Full, served in solarium and dining room
AMENITIES	Robes; complimentary wine & hors d'oeuvres, coffee, tea, & cookies
RESTRICTIONS	No smoking. No pets. Children over 12

PACIFIC GARDENS INN

701 Asilomar Blvd.   Pacific Grove, CA 93950   *(408) 646-9414*
Mary Nichols, Manager

LOCATION	Near Asilomar Beach. From Hwy. 68 follow signs to town, continue through 2 stop signs. Asilomar is 1/4 mi. past 2nd stop. Inn is on right
OPEN	All Year
DESCRIPTION	1986 Rustic-Shingle Contemporary furnishings
NO. OF ROOMS	28 w/private baths (Includes rooms, 1-bedroom suites w/queen beds & hide-a-bed, & 2-bedroom suites w/queen bed, double bed & hide-a-bed)
RATES	Rooms/$70-98 Mini Suites/$99-115 1-Bedroom Suites/$115-135 2-Bedroom Suites/$125-145 Reservation/cancellation policy
CREDIT CARDS	American Express, MasterCard, Visa
BREAKFAST	Continental, served in lobby area
AMENITIES	Two outdoor hot tubs; fireplace, TV/radio/phone, popcorn & poppers, & coffee makers in rooms; complimentary evening wine & cheese
RESTRICTIONS	None
RATED	AAA 3 Diamonds

ROSEROX COUNTRY INN BY-THE-SEA

557 Ocean View Blvd.   Pacific Grove, CA 93950   *(408) 373-7673*
Dawn Vyette Browncroft, Resident Owner

LOCATION	On the beach. From Hwy. 68 west, go 5 mi. to Ocean View Blvd., right 1 block to the corner of Grand Ave.
OPEN	All Year
DESCRIPTION	1904 4-story Country Victorian Country Victorian furnishings
NO. OF ROOMS	8 share 4 baths
RATES	Single/$105 Double/$125-205 Reservation/cancellation policy 2-night minimum stay on weekends
CREDIT CARDS	No
BREAKFAST	Full, served in Country French morning room, on ocean patio, or in bed
AMENITIES	Robes & down comforters; ocean views from all rooms; private parking; complimentary afternoon wine & cheese, & memento
RESTRICTIONS	No smoking. No pets
REVIEWED	*American Historic Bed & Breakfast Inns & Guesthouses* *Complete Guide to Bed & Breakfasts, Inns & Guesthouses*
MEMBER	California Lodging Industry Assn.

SEVEN GABLES INN

555 Ocean View Blvd.   Pacific Grove, CA 93950   *(408) 372-4341*
The Flatley Family, Resident Owners

LOCATION	On the ocean front. From Forest Ave., right on Ocean View Blvd. for 2 blocks
OPEN	All Year
DESCRIPTION	1886 3-story Formal Victorian Mansion Elegant Victorian antique furnishings
NO. OF ROOMS	14 w/private baths
RATES	$95-185 Reservation/cancellation policy 2-night minimum on weekends
CREDIT CARDS	MasterCard, Visa
BREAKFAST	Full, served in grand dining room
AMENITIES	Ocean views from all rooms; complimentary afternoon High Tea; limited handicapped access
RESTRICTIONS	No smoking. No pets (resident cat & dog). Children over 12
REVIEWED	*American Historic Bed & Breakfast Inns & Guesthouses* *America's Wonderful Little Hotels & Inns* *Bed & Breakfast Guide California* *Bed & Breakfast in California* *Best Places to Stay in California* *Complete Guide to Bed & Breakfasts, Inns & Guesthouses* *Country Inns & Back Roads: California* *Fodor's Bed & Breakfasts, Country Inns & Other Weekend Pleasures—The West Coast* *The National Trust Guide to Historic Bed & Breakfasts, Inns and Small Hotels*
MEMBER	California Assn. of B&B Inns
RATED	Mobil 3 Stars

PALM SPRINGS

This is the ultimate desert oasis, the land of 70 golf courses — one million gallons of recycled water a day keep them green — tennis courts, air conditioning, swimming pools and the very rich and famous. Winter is wonderful, the air is clear and pure and the night sky is to wonder at. Take in the Botanical Gardens, Desert Museum and the performing arts in the Annenberg Theater. Or rise 8,000 ft. via the Aerial Tramway to Mt. San Jancinto State Park and Wilderness Area for hiking and cross-country skiing. Or stay cool by the pool. From Los Angeles, about two hours southeast via I-10 and Hwy. 111.

CASA CODY BED & BREAKFAST COUNTRY INN

175 S. Cahuilla Dr.   Palm Springs, CA 92262   *(619) 320-9346*
Therese Hayes, Resident Owner   *(800) 231-2639   FAX: (619) 325-8610*

LOCATION	Hwy. 111 to Palm Canyon Dr., then west on Tahquitz Canyon, 2nd left (south) on Cahuilla Rd.
OPEN	All Year
DESCRIPTION	1920's California Hacienda Southwestern (Santa Fe) furnishings
NO. OF ROOMS	17 w/private baths
RATES	$45-160 (vary according to season) Reservation/cancellation policy 2-night minimum on weekends
CREDIT CARDS	American Express, MasterCard, Visa
BREAKFAST	Continental, served poolside
AMENITIES	2 swimming pools, hot tub; all rooms w/TV & phones, air conditioning & refrigerators, suites have fully equipped kitchens; 6 rooms w/fireplaces; small meeting facilities; handicapped access; Saturday complimentary wine & cheese
RESTRICTIONS	None
REVIEWED	*American Historic Bed & Breakfast Inns & Guesthouses* *America's Wonderful Little Hotels & Inns* *Bed & Breakfast in California* *Best Bed & Breakfasts & Country Inns: West* *California Country Inns & Itineraries* *Complete Guide to Bed & Breakfasts, Inns & Guesthouses* *Frommer's Los Angeles*
RATED	AAA 2 Diamonds Mobil 2 Stars

INGLESIDE INN

200 West Ramon Rd.   Palm Springs, CA 92264   (619) 325-0046
Melvyn Haber, Owner   800-772-6655   FAX: (619) 325-0710

LOCATION	From Hwy. 10 take exit 111, continue approx. 10 mi. to center of town, right on Ramon
OPEN	All Year
DESCRIPTION	1922 Country Estate with restaurant Deluxe eclectic furnishings
NO. OF ROOMS	28 w/private baths
RATES	Inquire Reservation/cancellation policy 2-night minimum on weekends
CREDIT CARDS	American Express, Discover, MasterCard, Visa
BREAKFAST	Continental, served in room, poolside, on veranda or private patio Lunch & dinner available in restaurant
AMENITIES	Swimming, hot tub, sauna; all rooms w/robes, TV/radios & phones, some w/fireplaces; complimentary cheese & fresh fruit, & champagne for special occasions; meeting facilities
RESTRICTIONS	None
REVIEWED	*American Historic Bed & Breakfast Inns & Guesthouses* *California Country Inns & Itineraries* *Complete Guide to Bed & Breakfasts, Inns & Guesthouses* *Country Inns & Back Roads: California* *Fodor's Bed & Breakfasts, Country Inns & Other Weekend Pleasures—* *The West Coast*

LE PETIT CHATEAU

1491 Via Soledad   Palm Springs, CA 92264   *(619) 325-2686*
Donald & Mary Robidoux, Resident Owners

LOCATION	1 mi. south of center of town. South Palm Canyon Dr. on corner of Avenida Palmera, then 1 block east to corner of Via Soledad
OPEN	All Year
DESCRIPTION	1952 walled & gated Mediterranean Villa French Country furnishings
NO. OF ROOMS	10 w/private baths
RATES	$90-130 Reservation/cancellation policy 2-night minimum on weekends
CREDIT CARDS	American Express, Diner's Club, Discover, MasterCard, Visa
BREAKFAST	Continental plus, served on patio
AMENITIES	Clothing-optional swimming pool & hot tub; private brick patios; mist tanning system; king & queen beds; some suites w/kitchens; TV/radio & phone in rooms; complimentary afternoon wine, cheese & fruit
RESTRICTIONS	No smoking. No pets. No children

ORCHID TREE INN

261 S. Belardo Rd.   Palm Springs, CA 92262   *(619) 325-2791*
Greg Strauss, Manager   *(800) 733-3435   FAX: (619) 325-3855*

LOCATION	From south Palm Canyon Dr., west on Arenas 1 block to Belardo, then south 1/2 block to Inn on west side of street
OPEN	All Year, B&B November 1-May 31 only
DESCRIPTION	1915-58 Eclectic array of suites, studios, and Spanish bungalows
NO. OF ROOMS	40 w/private baths
RATES	$50-250 Reservation/cancellation policy
CREDIT CARDS	American Express, MasterCard, Visa
BREAKFAST	Continental, served in main lodge
AMENITIES	2 swimming pools, 1 hot tub; TV/radio & phone in rooms, some w/fireplace & kitchen; complimentary coffee & tea; meeting facilities, limited handicapped access; non-smoking rooms available
RESTRICTIONS	No pets (resident cat). Inquire about children
RATED	AAA 2 Diamonds

SAKURA, JAPANESE BED & BREAKFAST INN

1677 N. Via Miraleste   PO Box 9403   Palm Springs, CA 92263
George & Fumiko Cebra, Resident Owners

(619) 327-0705
FAX: (619) 327- 6847

LOCATION	From Hwy. 111, proceed to Vista Chino (3rd traffic light), left to Via Miraleste (3rd street on right). Parking lot is on Vista Chino (right side), just before Via Miraleste
OPEN	All Year
DESCRIPTION	1940's Country Adobe Japanese furnishings
NO. OF ROOMS	5 w/shared baths
RATES	$45-75 Reservation/cancellation policy 2-night minimum stay on weekends
CREDIT CARDS	American Express
BREAKFAST	Full Japanese or American, served in dining room, guestroom or poolside. Japanese & vegetarian dinners available by request
AMENITIES	Swimming pool, hot tub, Japanese Kimonos & slippers; TV/radio in rooms; complimentary Japanese tea & snacks; Japanese accupressure massage (Shiatsu) available
RESTRICTIONS	No smoking. No pets
REVIEWED	*American Historic Bed & Breakfast Inns & Guesthouses* *Bed & Breakfast Homes Directory: West Coast* *Inn Places For Bed & Breakfast in the West*
RSO	B&B International B&B of Los Angeles California Houseguests International Eye Openers B&B Reservations Rent-A-Room International

PALOS VERDES

The amazing thing about LA is that you can travel an hour out of town and find a place like Palos Verdes with beautiful homes, superb views and private beaches. Simply amazing.

PACIFIC VIEW BED & BREAKFAST

4110 Palos Verdes Dr. S. Rancho Palos Verdes, CA 90274
Ann Booth, Resident Owner   *(310) 377-2860*

LOCATION	On the beach. From 110 Harbor Freeway south, left on Gaffey to 25th St., right for 2-1/2 mi. to corner of Schooner. Gate on left, house is on frontage road
OPEN	All Year
DESCRIPTION	1953 Beach House Casual furnishings
NO. OF ROOMS	2 w/private baths
RATES	$55-66 Reservation/cancellation policy
CREDIT CARDS	No
BREAKFAST	Continental plus, served in dining room or on ocean deck
AMENITIES	Private beach w/volleyball, paddle tennis & barbeque facilities; phone in 1 room; Los Angeles newspaper available
RESTRICTIONS	No smoking. No pets. Inquire about children
REVIEWED	*Bed & Breakfast North America* *Bed & Breakfast: Southern California*
RSO	B&B of Los Angeles Rent-A-Room International

PASADENA

Baronial estates and lush, landscaped gardens mix it up with the Rose Bowl Game and the Rose Parade; the prestigious California Institute of Technology; the Huntington Library, Art Gallery & Botanical Gardens; the Norton Simon Museum of Art, and Tournament House, William Wrigley's former mansion, headquarters of the Tournament of Roses Association. About 11 miles northeast of downtown Los Angeles in the San Gabriel Valley.

THE ARTISTS' INN

1038 Magnolia St. South Pasadena, CA 91030   (818) 799-5668
Janet Marangi, Owner Rich Siefert, Resident Manager   FAX: (818) 799-5668

LOCATION	Exit Hwy. 110 at Orange Grove, right 1 block to Magnolia, left 3 blocks on Magnolia
OPEN	All Year
DESCRIPTION	1895 2-story Midwestern Victorian Farmhouse Antique furnishings
NO. OF ROOMS	4 w/private baths
RATES	$90-100
CREDIT CARDS	MasterCard, Visa
BREAKFAST	Your choice of full gourmet, continental plus, or continental Served in dining room, guestrooms, or on porches Picnic lunch & dinner available
AMENITIES	Fireplace, books, games & puzzles in living room; fresh flowers in rooms; complimentary afternoon tea & pastries, fresh fruit, coffee & tea all day
RESTRICTIONS	No smoking. No pets (resident cat: "Boots"). Children over 8

PASO ROBLES
(SAN LUIS OBISPO CO.)

Vineyards, wineries, almond orchards blooming in spring, and the largest thoroughbred race horse farm in the world are here. So are some terrific events: Paderewski Festival in March; Paso Robles Wine Festival and Great Western Bicycle Rally in May; California Mid-State Fair in August, and Balloon Fest in September. Or sample the wines anytime. From San Luis Obispo, 21 miles north on Hwy 101. Very handy to Lake Nacimiento for boating and fishing.

COUNTRY GARDEN INN

2430 Genesco Rd.   Paso Robles, CA 93446   (805) 238-6639
Tia Chapman, Resident Owner

LOCATION	10 mi. east of Hwy. 101, via Creston to Genesco Rd. Directions provided on brochure
OPEN	All Year
DESCRIPTION	1990 California Ranch Eclectic furnishings On 20 acres
NO. OF ROOMS	3 w/private baths in guest wing of house
RATES	$75 Reservation/cancellation policy
CREDIT CARDS	No
BREAKFAST	Continental plus, served in Game Room
AMENITIES	Game room w/fireplace, TV/VCR, microwave, games & sitting area; utility room w/refrigerator, washer & dryer; radios in rooms; complimentary refreshments; meeting facilities; handicapped access
RESTRICTIONS	None. Resident pets: Doberman, Australian Sheepdog mix, & Siamese cat (not allowed in guest quarters)
RSO	Megan's Friends B&B Reservation Service

HILLTOP HOUSE

1550 Cumbre Rd.   Paso Robles, CA 93446   *(805) 237-0896*
Lynn Criss, Resident Owner

LOCATION	On a hilltop in the country. Directions sent w/reservation confirmation
OPEN	All Year
DESCRIPTION	Custom-built 2-story Contemporary Colonial Eclectic furnishings On 6 acres
NO. OF ROOMS	1 w/private bath 2 w/shared baths
RATES	Weekends/PB/$125 SB/$100 Weekdays/PB/$100 SB/$75 Reservation/cancellation policy, 2-night minimum stay on weekends
CREDIT CARDS	No
BREAKFAST	Full gourmet, served in dining room or gazebo
AMENITIES	Swimming pool, hot tub, gazebo & patios; terry robes; TV/radio in rooms; complimentary fruit basket & wine; mountain bikes available
RESTRICTIONS	No smoking. Inquire about pets (resident friendly Australian Sheepdog, "Rosie" & 3 fat cats). Children over 16

THE ROOJ HOME

(RSO)   *Reservations: (805) 544-4406   FAX: (805) 546-8642*

LOCATION	Inquire
OPEN	All Year
DESCRIPTION	1900s California Farmhouse on 40 acres w/cabin Eclectic furnishings
NO. OF ROOMS	1 w/private bath 1 w/shared bath
RATES	$75-85 Reservation/cancellation policy
CREDIT CARDS	No
BREAKFAST	Continental, provided in guest cabin kitchen
AMENITIES	Swimming pool
RESTRICTIONS	No smoking. No pets. No children
RSO	Megan's Friends B&B Reservation Service

RAMONA

(SAN DIEGO)

This small town on the outskirts of Cleveland National Forest is on the high road to Anza-Borrego Desert State Park and just down the road from Julian. The 1886 Woodwards Home and Museum is worth a visit. Northeast of San Diego and east of Escondido via I-15 and Hwy. 78.

LUCYS' ATTIC

760 Cedar St.   Ramona, CA 92065   *(619) 788-9543*
Luanne Corea, Resident Owner

LOCATION	Central (call for directions)
OPEN	All Year
DESCRIPTION	1965 2-story Farm House Antique & eclectic furnishings
NO. OF ROOMS	1 w/private bath 1 s/shared bath
RATES	PB/$65-80 SB/$50-65
CREDIT CARDS	No
BREAKFAST	Full, served in dining room
AMENITIES	Swimming pool; TV/radio & phone in rooms; complimentary afternoon beverages
RESTRICTIONS	No smoking. Resident dog
REVIEWED	*Bed & Breakfast: Southern California* *California Country Inns & Itineraries*

REDLANDS
(RIVERSIDE)

The University of Redlands occupies 130 acres of this lovely little town, known for its 350 carefully restored Victorian homes. Check out the Kimberly Crest and the amazing array of architectures. And yes, it was named for the color of its soil. San Bernardino County Museum and Mission San Gabriel are of interest.

MOREY MANSION

190 Terracina Blvd.   Redlands, CA 92373
Leona Connell, Manager

(909) 793-7970
FAX: (909) 793-7870

LOCATION	Exit I-10 at Alabama, south to Barton Rd., right to Terracina Blvd., left to Mansion
OPEN	All Year
DESCRIPTION	1890 3-story Victorian with Russian/Moorish, Chinese, English & Italian influences Antique Victorian furnishings National Historic Register
NO. OF ROOMS	3 w/private baths 2 w/shared bath
RATES	PB/Weekday/$119-145 Weekend/$145-185 SB/Weekday/$109-119 Weekend/$125-145 Reservation/cancellation policy 2 night minimum stay on some weekends & holidays Inquire about extended stay rates
CREDIT CARDS	American Express, MasterCard, Visa
BREAKFAST	Continental, served in dining room or guestrooms
AMENITIES	TV in all rooms, fireplaces in 2 rooms; complimentary beverages available on request; wedding facilities
RESTRICTIONS	No smoking. No pets
REVIEWED	*American Historic Bed & Breakfast Inns & Guesthouses* *Bed & Breakfast in California* *Bed & Breakfast: Southern California* *Complete Guide to Bed & Breakfasts, Inns & Guesthouses*

REDONDO BEACH

One of the booming string of beach communities in the South Bay area populated by a good number of surfers. The 2,000-boat Kings Harbor and Fisherman's Warf pier are a maze of trendy shops, restaurants and even a concert auditorium. The International Surf Festival in August packs the wide beach.

BINDING HOSPITALITY BED & BREAKFAST

122 S. Juanita Ave.   Redondo Beach, CA 90277   *(310) 316-5123*
Betty & Norris Binding, Resident Owners

LOCATION	Directions provided on brochure
OPEN	June-April
DESCRIPTION	1987 Home Eclectic furnishings
NO. OF ROOMS	1 w/private bath & kitchenette
RATES	$35-45 Reservation/cancellation policy 2-night minimum stay Discount for stay of 1 week or more
CREDIT CARDS	No
BREAKFAST	Continental plus, provided in room
AMENITIES	Jacuzzi; robes & TV in room; complimentary fresh fruit
RESTRICTIONS	No smoking. No pets. Children over 5

REEDLEY

The Kings River runs through this rural gem, 40 miles from the Kings Canyon National Park. Don't miss the chance to see the Mennonite quilters at work at the Mennonite Quilting Center. And the Reedley Museum exhibits memorabilia of old-fashioned country living. Down at Kelley's Beach, there's tubing, canoeing and cooling off. From Fresno, 45 miles southeast via Hwy. 180 and Hwy. 63.

REEDLEY COUNTRY INN BED & BREAKFAST

43137 Rd. 52   Reedley, CA 93654   *(209) 638-2585*
George & Linda Penner, Resident Owners

LOCATION	Inquire
OPEN	All Year
DESCRIPTION	1988 English Tudor English Tudor furnishings
NO. OF ROOMS	4 w/private baths
RATES	$55-77 Reservation/cancellation policy
CREDIT CARDS	MasterCard, Visa
BREAKFAST	Full, served in Christian Brothers guest house
AMENITIES	TV/radio & phones in rooms; private patios; complimentary refreshments on request; meeting facilities; handicapped access
RESTRICTIONS	No smoking. No pets. Children 7 & over
REVIEWED	*Bed & Breakfast: Southern California*

RUNNING SPRINGS

In the San Bernardino Mountains, at the junction of Hwy. 330 and the Rim of the World Drive, this is the perfect jumping-off place to Lake Arrowhead, Big Bear Lake and everything in between.

SPRING OAKS BED & BREAKFAST INN

2465 Spring Oak Dr.   PO Box 2918   Running Springs, CA 92382
William & Laura Florian, Resident Owner   *(909) 867-9636*

LOCATION	Call for directions
OPEN	All Year
DESCRIPTION	1950 3-story Country Mountain Home Elegant country furnishings
NO. OF ROOMS	1 w/private bath 2 w/shared bath
RATES	PB/$120-130 SB/$85-95 Reservation/cancellation policy
CREDIT CARDS	MasterCard, Visa
BREAKFAST	Full, served in breakfast nook
AMENITIES	Hot tub, robes; live in-house concerts; complimentary afternoon wine & cheese; meeting facilities
RESTRICTIONS	No smoking. No pets (resident dog & cat). No children
REVIEWED	*Bed & Breakfast Homes Directory: West Coast* *Bed & Breakfast: Southern California*

SAN CLEMENTE

Remember when...the Western White House was here and Richard Nixon paced the beaches? His Casa Pacifica can still be seen atop the cliffs. Beyond its politics, this is one of Southern California's best seaside playgrounds and San Clemente State Beach is one of the least crowded and most beautiful. Cyclists will rejoyce at the 20-mile stretch to Camp Pendleton, where you are also welcome to ride. On Hwy. 101, near the northwest entrance to the Marine Corps. base.

CASA DE FLORES BED & BREAKFAST

184 Avenida La Cuesta   San Clemente, CA 92672   *(714) 498-1344*
Marilee Arsenault, Resident Owner

LOCATION	From the north: left on Palizada, left on Caballeros (becomes El Oriente), left on De La Paz/Avenida La Cuesta, 7th house on right
	From the south: left on Persidio, under freeway, right on Estrella, right on Palizada, under freeway, left on Caballeros (becomes El Oriente), left on De La Paz/Avenida La Cuesta, 7th house on the right
OPEN	All Year
DESCRIPTION	1974 2-Story Spanish Eclectic furnishings
NO. OF ROOMS	2 2-room suites w/private baths
RATES	$80-110 Reservation/cancellation policy 2-night minimum on weekends & holidays
CREDIT CARDS	No
BREAKFAST	Full, served in dining room
AMENITIES	Hot tub, robes; sand chairs & beach towels; full front veranda; orchid gardens; pool table; video games & movies; TV/radio in both suites, 1 w/fireplace; complimentary beverages & fruit; guest refrigerator
RESTRICTIONS	Smoking limited. No pets (resident cat, "J.J." & duck, "Chuckles")
REVIEWED	*Bed & Breakfast U.S.A.*
RSO	B&B of Los Angeles
MEMBER	Professional Assn. of Innkeepers International

CASA TROPICANA BED & BREAKFAST INN

610 Avenida Victoria   San Clemente, CA 92672   *(714) 492-1234*
Rick & Christy Anderson, Resident Owners

LOCATION	Beach-front across from San Clemente Pier. Exit I-5 at Ave. Palizadia, right to El Camino Real, left to Del Mar, right to pier
OPEN	All Year
DESCRIPTION	1990 4-story Spanish Inn with restaurant Eclectic furnishings w/tropical motif
NO. OF ROOMS	9 w/private baths
RATES	May 1-October 30: $75-350 November 1-April 30: $75-325 Reservation/cancellation policy 2-night minimum on weekends
CREDIT CARDS	All major cards
BREAKFAST	Full, served on ocean-view decks, in restaurant, or guestrooms Lunch & dinner available in restaurant
AMENITIES	All rooms w/queen & king beds, most w/fireplaces & jacuzzi tubs, 2 w/kitchenettes, 4 w/ocean views, some w/private decks; penthouse w/outdoor jacuzzi & 180 degree view
RESTRICTIONS	No smoking. No pets. No children
REVIEWED	*Bed & Breakfast: Southern California* *Best Places to Stay in California* *California Country Inns & Itineraries* *Complete Guide to Bed & Breakfasts, Inns & Guesthouses* *Fodor's Bed & Breakfasts, Country Inns & Other Weekend Pleasures—* *The West Coast* *Inn Places for Bed & Breakfast* *Special Places for the Discerning Traveler*

SAN DIEGO

Feel the sun, smell the ocean breeze and revel in the beauty. This is the state's second largest city and its County is the nation's 7th largest spreading from the desert, along 70 miles of coastline and ending at the Mexican border. Among the many notables not to miss: Cabrillo National Monument; Maritime Museum; Balboa Park and San Siego Zoo; Scripps Aquarium, and shopping at Horton Plaza or across the border in Tijuana. Some fun events: San Diego Crew Classic in Mission May in April; Miramar's Naval Air Show in July; Dixieland Jazz Festival on Thanksgiving weekend; and the Sea World Holiday Bowl in December. You really just have to be there.

BALBOA PARK INN

3402 Park Blvd.   San Diego, CA 92103
Ed Wilcox, Manager

(619) 298-0823
FAX: (619) 294-8070

LOCATION	In residential neighborhood on north edge of Balboa Park (short walk from San Diego Zoo). Exit Hwy. 5 at Hwy. 163, north to Richmond, right on Upas St. to corner of Park Blvd.
OPEN	All Year
DESCRIPTION	1915 Complex of 4 Spanish Colonial Buildings Eclectic furnishings
NO. OF ROOMS	25 suites w/private baths
RATES	$75-175 Reservation/cancellation policy Inquire about minimum stay during holidays
CREDIT CARDS	MasterCard, Visa
BREAKFAST	Continental plus, served in courtyard, sun terrace or suites
AMENITIES	All suites have sitting area, queen-sized bed, refrigerator, HBO cable TV, telephone w/complimentary local calls; some suites have kitchens, jacuzzi tubs, fireplaces, private decks, patios & wet bars; complimentary wine for special occasions; wedding/reception facilities
RESTRICTIONS	No pets
REVIEWED	*American Historic Bed & Breakfast Inns & Guesthouses* *Best Places to Stay in California* *Complete Guide to Bed & Breakfasts, Inns & Guesthouses* *Fodor's Bed & Breakfast Guide*
RATED	Mobil 4 Stars

BARROW'S BED & BREAKFAST

(RSO)	*Reservations: (415) 696-1690 FAX: (415) 696-1699*

LOCATION	In Mission Hills
OPEN	All Year
DESCRIPTION	1920s Spanish Adobe Some antique & eclectic furnishings
NO. OF ROOMS	1 w/private bath
RATES	$55 Reservation/cancellation policy 2-night minimum stay
CREDIT CARDS	MasterCard, Visa
BREAKFAST	Full, served in dining room
RESTRICTIONS	No smoking. No pets (resident large dogs)
RSO	B&B International

BETTY S. BED & BREAKFAST

3742 Arizona St. San Diego, CA 92104	*(619) 692-1385*
Betty Spiva Simpson, Resident Owner	

LOCATION	Near downtown & Balboa Park, 1-1/2 blocks south of University Ave., 1 block east of Texas St.
OPEN	All Year
DESCRIPTION	1912 California Bungalow Contemporary & some antique furnishings
NO. OF ROOMS	3 rooms share 2 baths
RATES	$25-35 Reservation/cancellation policy Inquire about long term rates
CREDIT CARDS	No
BREAKFAST	Full, served in dining room
AMENITIES	Family room w/TV/VCR/tape player/recorder; TV/radio & phone in rooms; occasional complimentary refreshments; laundry facilities available; limited handicapped access; bus, train or plane pickup available for extra charge
RESTRICTIONS	No smoking. No pets (resident dog). No children
MEMBER	Tourist House Assn. of America

CAROLE'S BED & BREAKFAST INN

3227 Grim Ave.   San Diego, CA 92104   (619) 280-5258
Carole Dugdale & Michael O'Brien, Resident Owners

LOCATION	I-5 south to Pershing, then Redwood to Grim (all one-way streets)
OPEN	All Year
DESCRIPTION	1904 2-story California Bungalow Turn-of-the-century w/some antique & reproduction furnishings
NO. OF ROOMS	1 w/private bath 3 w/shared baths
RATES	PB/$60-70 SB/$55-60 Reservation/cancellation policy
CREDIT CARDS	No
BREAKFAST	Continental plus, served in dining room, kitchen or on patio Lunch & dinner available
AMENITIES	Swimming pool, hot tub; TV/radio in rooms, phone available on request; complimentary wine & cheese
RESTRICTIONS	Smoking limited. No pets. Children over 10
REVIEWED	*The Annual Directory of American Bed & Breakfasts* *Bed & Breakfast Homes Directory: West Coast* *Complete Guide to Bed & Breakfasts, Inns & Guesthouses*

COATE'S

(RSO)   Reservations: (415) 696-1690   FAX: (415) 696-1699

LOCATION	In Mission Hills Old Town section
OPEN	All Year
DESCRIPTION	1920s Spanish Elegant furnishings
NO. OF ROOMS	1 w/shared bath
RATES	$55 Reservation/cancellation policy 2-night minimum stay
CREDIT CARDS	MasterCard, Visa
BREAKFAST	Full, served in dining room
RESTRICTIONS	No smoking. No pets (resident cat)
RSO	B&B International

THE COTTAGE

3829 Albatross St. San Diego, CA 92103   *(619) 299-1564*
Carol & Robert Emerick, Resident Owners

LOCATION	In the Hillcrest area, 1-1/2 mi. from San Diego Zoo. Exit I-5 south at Washington, left half-way up hill to University; right 9 blocks to Front St., right 1 block to Robinson, right 1 block to Albatross.
OPEN	All Year
DESCRIPTION	1913 2-story Redwood Homestead & Cottage Antique furnishings
NO. OF ROOMS	1 cottage w/private bath, living room & fully equipped kitchen 1 room in main house w/private bath & entrance
RATES	Cottage/$65-75 Room/$49 Reservation/cancellation policy 2-night minimum stay
CREDIT CARDS	American Express, MasterCard, Visa
BREAKFAST	Continental, served in cottage & main house dining room
AMENITIES	King & queen beds, TV/radio & phone in rooms
RESTRICTIONS	No smoking. No pets
REVIEWED	*American Historic Bed & Breakfast Inns & Guesthouses* *America's Wonderful Little Hotels & Inns* *Annual Directory of American Bed & Breakfast* *Bed & Breakfast Homes Directory: West Coast* *Bed & Breakfast in California* *Bed & Breakfast: Southern California* *Bed & Breakfast U.S.A.* *Best Places to Stay in California* *Complete Guide to Bed & Breakfasts, Inns & Guesthouses* *Frommer's San Diego*
RSO	Eye Openers B&B Reservations
MEMBER	American B&B Assn. B&B Guild of San Diego
RATED	ABBA 3 Crowns

ERENE'S BED & BREAKFAST

3776 Hawk St.   San Diego, CA 92103   (619) 295-5622
Erene Rallis, Resident Owner

LOCATION	In Mission Hills. Left on Harbor to Laural St., left to State St. which becomes Goldfinch, left on Sutter, right on Hawk
OPEN	All Year
DESCRIPTION	1910 Mission Hills cedar cottage Antique furnishings
NO. OF ROOMS	1 w/private bath 1 w/shared bath
RATES	$39.50-49.50 Reservation/cancellation policy
CREDIT CARDS	No
BREAKFAST	Weekends/Full, served in dining room Weekdays/Continental, served in dining room Inquire about dinner
AMENITIES	Living room w/fireplace; robes, TV/radio, fresh flowers & fruit in rooms; complimentary beverages on arrival; small meeting facilities
RESTRICTIONS	No smoking. Inquire about pets. No children

HARBOR HILL GUEST HOUSE

2330 Albatross St.   San Diego, CA 92101   (619) 233-0638
Dorothy A. Milbourn, Resident Owner

LOCATION	Just off I-5, near Balboa Park
OPEN	All Year
DESCRIPTION	1920s 3-story Traditional Home & Carriage House Eclectic furnishings
NO. OF ROOMS	5 rooms w/private baths
RATES	$65-85 Reservation/cancellation policy
CREDIT CARDS	MasterCard, Visa
BREAKFAST	Continental, provided in suite
AMENITIES	Decks & harbor views, cable TV/radio, phone & ceiling fans in rooms; kitchens & private entrances on each level, complimentary refreshments
RESTRICTIONS	Smoking limited. No pets

HERITAGE PARK BED & BREAKFAST INN

2470 Heritage Park Row
San Diego, CA 92110
Nancy & Charles Helsper, Resident Owners

(800) 995-2470
(619) 299-6832
FAX: (619) 299-9465

LOCATION	In Old Town Historic District. Exit I-5 at Old Town Ave., left on San Diego Ave., right on Harney into Heritage Park
OPEN	All Year
DESCRIPTION	1889 3-Story Queen Anne Victorian on a 7.8 acre park Wraparound veranda Victorian furnishings National Historic Register
NO. OF ROOMS	4 w/private baths 4 w/shared bath
RATES	PB/Sgl/$70-115 Dbl/$75-120 SB/Sgl/$60-105 Dbl/$65-110 2-night minimum stay on weekends
CREDIT CARDS	MasterCard, Visa
BREAKFAST	Full, served in dining room or on veranda Private gourmet candlelight dinners available
AMENITIES	Terry robes, radio & fresh flowers in all rooms, some w/fireplaces & private entrances; phones available; complimentary evening social hour; vintage classic films shown nightly; meeting facilities; handicapped access; turn-down service & pillow chocolates
RESTRICTIONS	No smoking. No pets
REVIEWED	American Historic Bed & Breakfast Inns & Guesthouses Bed & Breakfast in California Bed & Breakfast: Southern California California Country Inns & Itineraries Complete Guide to Bed & Breakfasts, Inns & Guesthouses Country Inns & Back Roads: California Fodor's Bed & Breakfasts, Country Inns & Other Weekend Pleasures— The West Coast
MEMBER	B&B Inns of Southern California Professional Assn. of Innkeepers International
RATED	ABBA 3 Crowns Mobil 3 Stars

HILL HOUSE BED & BREAKFAST INN

2504 A Street   San Diego, CA 92102   *(619) 239-4738*
Russ Atwater, Resident Owner

LOCATION	In Golden Hill Historic District. Exit I-5 at Pershing Dr., right at light onto 26th St., up hill to A Street, right to end of block (on corner of 25th)
OPEN	All Year
DESCRIPTION	1904 2-story Dutch Colonial Craftsman Victorian furnishings
NO. OF ROOMS	4 share 3 baths 1 suite w/private bath, living room, kitchen & private sunporch 1 cottage w/private bath & entrance, living room, kitchen & courtyard garden
RATES	PB/$85 SB/$55-75 Reservation/cancellation policy 2-night minimum on weekends Inquire about weekly & special rates
CREDIT CARDS	MasterCard, Visa
BREAKFAST	Full, served in formal dining room Gourmet & country picnic baskets available w/prior notice
AMENITIES	All rooms w/sitting areas, queen beds, robes & TV/radio, 1 w/fireplace; fireplace & phone in parlor; complimentary beverages & afternoon snacks
RESTRICTIONS	No smoking. No pets (resident dog "Trebor"). Children over 12
AWARDS	1991 Golden Hill Hospitality $ Revitalization Award
REVIEWED	*Bed & Breakfast: Southern California* *Frommer's '93 Bed & Breakfast: North America*
RSO	B&B International B&B of Southern California
MEMBER	B&B Guild of San Diego

KEATING HOUSE INN

2331 2nd Ave.   San Diego, CA 92101   *(619) 239-8585*
Ruth Babb, Manager

LOCATION	Exit I-5 at Sassafras, 1.1 mi. to Laurel, left & up hill to 2nd St., left 1-1/2 blocks to Inn
OPEN	All Year
DESCRIPTION	1888 2-story Queen Anne Victorian Victorian furnishings
NO. OF ROOMS	2 w/private baths 6 w/shared baths
RATES	PB/$70-80 SB/$60-80 Reservation/cancellation policy 2 night minimum during holidays
CREDIT CARDS	American Express, Discover, MasterCard, Visa
BREAKFAST	Full, served in dining room
AMENITIES	Radios in all rooms, fireplace in 1 room; complimentary beverages
RESTRICTIONS	Smoking limited. No pets
REVIEWED	*American Historic Bed & Breakfast Inns & Guesthouses* *America's Wonderful Little Hotels & Inns* *Bed & Breakfast Guide California* *Bed & Breakfast in California* *Bed & Breakfast: Southern California* *Complete Guide to Bed & Breakfasts, Inns & Guesthouses* *Hidden Coast of California*
MEMBER	California Assn. of Bed & Breakfast Inns B&B Guild of San Diego

SAN JACINTO
(RIVERSIDE)

Just on the outskirts of Hemet, this is a good place to be in April and May, the time of the renown Ramona Pageant. Based on Helen Hunt Jackson's 1884 novel, the revival has been presented annually since 1923, with 350 participants. This is one of the state's greatest outdoor spectacles. Write way ahead for tickets. 35 miles southeast of Riverside via Hwys. 215 and 74.

VIRGINIA LEE HOTEL

248 E. Main St. San Jacinto, CA 92583   *(909) 654-2270*
Al & Virginia Thompson, Resident Owners

LOCATION	From Hwy. 79, right on San Jacinto St., left on Main St.
OPEN	All Year
DESCRIPTION	1884 2-story Western Hotel with Gift Shop Some antique & eclectic furnishings
NO. OF ROOMS	2 w/private baths 7 w/shared bath
RATES	PB/$50 SB/$45
CREDIT CARDS	No
BREAKFAST	Continental, served in Al's Coffee Spot
AMENITIES	Full front balcony; early-bird coffee; hot & cold drinks in rooms; ice & room fans available; garden; meeting facilities
RESTRICTIONS	No smoking. No pets (resident dog). No children
REVIEWED	*Bed & Breakfast in California*

SAN LUIS OBISPO

In the heart of central California wine country, backdropped by the Santa Lucia Mountains and 12 miles inland from the coast on Hwy. 101. California State Polytechnic University is here and the Mission San Luis Obispo. Major events include the acclaimed Mozart Festival in July-August and Central Coast Wine Festival in September. And on Thursday nights, the Farmer's Market offers up fresh produce, barbequed ribs and fresh fish, street dancers and puppeteers. To pick your own goodies, ask the Chamber of Commerce about the farm trails program. Handy to Los Osos Oaks State Reserve.

ADOBE INN

1473 Monterey St.   San Luis Obispo, CA 93401   *(805) 549-0321*
Michael & Ann Dinshaw, Resident Owners

LOCATION	Exit Hwy. 101 at California St., turn left & at 2nd traffic signal turn right onto Monterey. From Hwy. 1 turn left onto Monterey St.
OPEN	All Year
DESCRIPTION	1950s 2-story Inn Southwestern furnishings
NO. OF ROOMS	15 w/private baths
RATES	Sgl/$40-80 Dbl/$45-85 Reservation/cancellation policy Inquire about 2-night minimum stay
CREDIT CARDS	American Express, Discover, MasterCard, Visa
BREAKFAST	Full buffet, served in breakfast room Afternoon tea available
AMENITIES	Early-bird coffee; cable TV/radio & phone in rooms, some w/window seats; small meeting facilities; Hearst Castle tours arranged
RESTRICTIONS	Smoking limited. No pets
REVIEWED	*Complete Guide to Bed & Breakfasts, Inns & Guesthouses* *Let's Go: The Budget Guide to California & Hawaii* *On the Loose in California, Las Vegas & The Grand Canyon*
MEMBER	National B&B Assn.
RATED	Mobil Quality Rating

GARDEN STREET INN

1212 Garden St.   San Luis Obispo, CA 93401   *(805) 545-9802*
Dan & Kathy Smith, Resident Owners

LOCATION	Off Hwy. 101 at Marsh St., go 6 blocks, right on Garden St., large grey Victorian on left
OPEN	All Year
DESCRIPTION	1887 restored 2-story Italianate/Queen Anne Victorian & eclectic furnishings California Historic Register
NO. OF ROOMS	9 rooms & 4 suites w/private baths
RATES	Rooms/$90-120 Suites/$140-160 Reservation/cancellation policy 2-night minimum during holidays & special event weekends
CREDIT CARDS	American Express, MasterCard, Visa
BREAKFAST	Full, served in McCaffrey Morning Room or in guestrooms
AMENITIES	Hot tub; all rooms w/queen or king beds, robes, armories, fireplaces, radios & phones, some w/jacuzzi tubs & private decks; complimentary evening wine & hors d'oeuvres; library; small meeting facilities; limited handicapped access
RESTRICTIONS	No smoking. No pets (resident Lhasa Apso/Cocker "Mozart") Inquire about children
REVIEWED	*American Historic Bed & Breakfast Inns & Guesthouses* *Annual Directory of American Bed & Breakfast* *Bed & Breakfast: Southern California* *Complete Guide to Bed & Breakfasts, Inns & Guesthouses* *Fodor's Bed & Breakfasts, Country Inns, & Other Weekend Pleasures—* *The West* *Inn Places for Bed & Breakfast* *Inspected, Rated & Approved Bed & Breakfasts & Country Inns*
RSO	B&B International Eye Openers B&B Reservations
MEMBER	Special Places
RATED	AAA 3 Diamonds ABBA 3 Crowns

HERITAGE INN

978 Olive St.   San Luis Obispo, CA 93401   (805) 544-7440
Zella Harrison, Resident Owner

LOCATION	Creekside. Exit Hwy. 101 south at Santa Rosa St., then 100 yds. on left
OPEN	All Year
DESCRIPTION	1903 2-story Victorian Period antique furnishings National Historic Register
NO. OF ROOMS	3 w/private baths 6 w/shared baths
RATES	PB/$76-86 SB/$66-76 Reservation/cancellation policy
CREDIT CARDS	MasterCard, Visa
BREAKFAST	Continental plus, served in dining room
AMENITIES	Fireplaces in dining room & parlor; robes; 3 rooms w/vanity/sink areas; complimentary wine, & hors d'oeuvres, & bedtime candy; small meeting facilities; handicapped access
RESTRICTIONS	No smoking. No pets. Children over 12
REVIEWED	*American Historic Bed & Breakfast Inns & Guesthouses* *Bed & Breakfast in California* *Complete Guide to Bed & Breakfasts, Inns & Guesthouses*

HOMESTAY

(RSO)   Reservations: (805) 544-4406   FAX: (805) 546-8642

LOCATION	Inquire
OPEN	All Year
DESCRIPTION	Contemporary Home Eclectic furnishings
NO. OF ROOMS	1 w/shared bath
RATES	$50 Reservation/cancellation policy Minimum stay during holiday weekends
CREDIT CARDS	No
BREAKFAST	Full, served in dining room
RESTRICTIONS	No smoking. No pets (resident cat). No children
RSO	Megan's Friends B&B Reservation Service

SAN PEDRO

Worldport Los Angeles is here, one of the largest deepwater ports in the nation. Watch the ships, or try a harbor cruise on a square-rigged sailing ship. This is the major access terminal for Catalina Island, and Fort McArthur overlooks the harbor. Visit Ports O' Call Village, the Maritime and Cabrillo Marine Museums and see the Christmas Afloat Parade in December. On the Palos Verdes Peninsula immediately west of Long beach via I-405, I-110 and Hwy. 1.

THE GRAND COTTAGES

815-829 S. Grand Ave. San Pedro, CA 90731   (310) 548-1240/519-1156
Mailing address: 325 W. 7th St. San Pedro, CA 90731   FAX: (310) 514-2279
Barbeur Wise, Manager

LOCATION	In Wharf Town. At end of Freeway 110 south, turn left on Gaffey St., left on 9th St., left on Grand Ave.
OPEN	All Year
DESCRIPTION	1930s Bungalows Eclectic furnishings
NO. OF ROOMS	4 cottages w/private baths, bedrooms, living rooms, kitchens, back patios & front porches
RATES	Sgl/$75 Dbl/$90 Reservation/cancellation policy
CREDIT CARDS	American Express, MasterCard, Visa
BREAKFAST	Continental, provided in cottages Lunch & dinner available next door at The Grand House
AMENITIES	TV/VCR/radio, phones & complimentary bottle of champagne in all cottages, 3 w/fireplaces; private parking
RESTRICTIONS	No smoking. No pets (resident outdoor cat). Limit of 3 persons per cottage
REVIEWED	*American Historic Bed & Breakfast Inns & Guesthouses* *Bed & Breakfast in California* *Complete Guide to Bed & Breakfasts, Inns & Guesthouses*
MEMBER	B&B Innkeepers of Southern California

SANTA BARBARA

Its historic Spanish influence is everywhere: whitewashed architecture, splendid missions and the week-long Old Days Fiesta in August not to mention spectacular coastline and beaches, too. Go see Sterns Wharf for things to do, or just the view. On a clear day, look past the oil rigs to the Channel Islands. From here the Nature Conservancy leads tours to Santa Cruz, the largest of the islands. The Andre Clark Bird Refuge is worth a visit as is El Presidio and the every-Sunday Arts and Crafts show. In October, the International Jazz Festival is one to plan for. Very handy to Solvang. On the Central Coast via Hwy. 101.

BATH STREET INN

1720 Bath St.   Santa Barbara, CA 93101   *(805) 682-9680*
Susan Brown, Resident Owner   *FAX: (800) 766-2284*

LOCATION	Exit Hwy. 101 at Carrillo St., east to Bath St., north to Inn
OPEN	All Year
DESCRIPTION	1890 3-story Queen Anne Victorian Victorian furnishings
NO. OF ROOMS	8 w/private baths
RATES	Sgl/$90 Dbl/$115 Reservation/cancellation policy 2-night minimum on weekends
CREDIT CARDS	American Express, MasterCard, Visa
BREAKFAST	Full, served in dining room or garden patio
AMENITIES	Library & TV lounge; radio in rooms; fresh flowers & complimentary evening refreshments; complimentary use of bicycles; handicapped access
RESTRICTIONS	No smoking. No pets (resident Golden Retriever/Lab)
REVIEWED	*American Historic Bed & Breakfast Inns & Guesthouses* *America's Wonderful Little Hotels & Inns* *Bed & Breakfast in California* *Bed & Breakfast: Southern California* *Complete Guide to Bed & Breakfasts, Inns & Guesthouses* *Country Inns & Back Roads: California* *Fodor's Bed & Breakfasts, Country Inns & Other Weekend Pleasures—* * The West Coast* *Frommer's California*
MEMBER	B&B Innkeepers of Southern California Santa Barbara Innkeepers Guild
RATED	AAA 2 Diamonds

THE BAYBERRY INN BED & BREAKFAST

111 W. Valerio St.   Santa Barbara, CA 93101   *(805) 682-3199*
Keith Pomeroy, Resident Owner   *(800) 528-9691   FAX: (805) 962-0103*

LOCATION	Exit Hwy. 101 at Mission St., east (towards mountains) to De La Vina St., right 3 blocks to Valerio, left to end of block. Inn is on the right
OPEN	All Year (Closed December 24 & 25)
DESCRIPTION	1886 2-story Modified Federal post-Victorian furnishings
NO. OF ROOMS	8 w/private baths
RATES	$85-135 Reservation/cancellation policy 2-night minimum stay on weekends Inquire about minimum stay during holidays & midweek rates
CREDIT CARDS	American Express, Discover, MasterCard, Visa
BREAKFAST	Full, served in dining room or garden
AMENITIES	Gardens w/croquet & badminton; all rooms w/canopied beds, down comforters & pillows, TV/radios, some w/fireplaces; phone in rooms by request; guest refrigerator; complimentary afternoon tea & snacks, & morning newspapers; small meeting facilities
RESTRICTIONS	No smoking. Inquire about pets
REVIEWED	*American Historic Bed & Breakfast Inns & Guesthouses* *Annual Directory of American Bed & Breakfast* *Bed & Breakfast in California* *Bed & Breakfast: Southern California* *Best Places to Stay in California* *Complete Guide to Bed & Breakfasts, Inns & Guesthouses* *Country Inns & Back Roads: California* *Country Inns, Lodges & Historic Hotels of California, Oregon & Washington* *Fodor's Bed & Breakfasts, Country Inns & Other Weekend Pleasures— The West Coast* *Inn Places for Bed & Breakfast*
MEMBER	B&B Innkeepers of Southern California Professional Assn. of Innkeepers International Santa Barbara B&B Innkeepers Guild
RATED	AAA 2 Diamonds

BED & BREAKFAST AT VALLI'S VIEW

340 N. Sierra Vista Rd.   Santa Barbara, CA 93108   *(805) 969-1272*
Valli & Larry Stevens, Resident Owners

LOCATION	On top of Eucalyptus Hill, in the foothills of Montecito, 3 mi. northeast of town. Map sent with deposit receipt
OPEN	All Year
DESCRIPTION	1979 California Ranch Eclectic furnishings
NO. OF ROOMS	1 w/private bath
RATES	$70-75 Reservation/cancellation policy 2-night minimum on weekends
CREDIT CARDS	No
BREAKFAST	Full, served in dining room or on patio
AMENITIES	Large deck, fern garden, & patio, robes, TV/radio in rooms; complimentary refreshments; handicapped access
RESTRICTIONS	No smoking. No pets (resident outside cats)
REVIEWED	*The Annual Directory of American Bed & Breakfast* *Bed & Breakfast Homes Directory: West Coast* *Bed & Breakfast North America* *Official Bed & Breakfast Guide for the U.S.*

BLUE QUAIL INN & COTTAGES BED & BREAKFAST

1908 Bath St. Santa Barbara, CA 93101	CA (800) 549-1622
Jeanise Suding Eaton, Resident Owner	USA (800) 676-1622
	(805) 687- 2300

LOCATION	Exit Hwy. 101 at Mission St., east 1 block to Castillo, right 1 block to Pedregosa St., left 1 block to Bath St., right 1/2 block to Inn
OPEN	All Year (Closed December 24 & 25)
DESCRIPTION	1915 California Bungalow & 4 Cottages English & American Country furnishings
NO. OF ROOMS	2 rooms in main house 3 rooms & 3 suites in cottages 1 private cottage, w/private baths
RATES	Rooms in main house/$82 Rooms in cottages/$95 Suites in cottages/$95-115 Private cottage/$165 Reservation/cancellation policy 2-night minimum on weekends
CREDIT CARDS	American Express, MasterCard, Visa
BREAKFAST	Full, served in main house dining room or on garden patio Picnic lunches available
AMENITIES	Private entrances; all rooms w/fireplaces & radios; complimentary afternoon wine & hors d'oeuvres, & evening sweets & hot spiced cider; meeting facilities; complimentary use of bicycles
RESTRICTIONS	No smoking. No pets (resident Cocker Spaniels)
REVIEWED	*American Historic Bed & Breakfast Inns & Guesthouses* *America's Wonderful Little Hotels & Inns* *The Annual Directory of American Bed & Breakfast* *Bed & Breakfast in California* *Bed & Breakfast: Southern California* *Best Places to Stay in California* *Complete Guide to Bed & Breakfasts, Inns & Guesthouses* *Inspected, Rated & Approved Bed & Breakfasts & Country Inns* *The National Trust Guide to Historic Bed & Breakfasts, Inns & Small Hotels* *The Non-Smoker's Guide to Bed & Breakfast*
MEMBER	American B&B Assn. B&B Innkeepers of Southern California National B&B Assn. Santa Barbara B&B Innkeepers Guild
RATED	AAA 2 Diamonds ABBA 2 Crowns

CASA DEL MAR INN

18 Bath St.   Santa Barbara, CA 93101   *(800) 433-3097   (805) 963-4418*
Rebecca Montgomery, Resident Owner   *FAX: (805) 966-4240*

LOCATION	1/2 block from beach & harbor
	South bound: Exit Hwy. 101 at Castillo, right for 4 blocks, left on Cabrillo Blvd. for 1 block, left on Bath
	North bound: Exit Hwy. 101 at Cabrillo, left 2.2 mi. to Bath, turn right
OPEN	All Year
DESCRIPTION	1929 & 1950 2-story Mediterranean Hotel
	Eclectic furnishings
NO. OF ROOMS	20 w/private baths
	(Includes 1 or 2 room family suites w/kitchen & fireplace, deluxe king rooms, or single rooms)
RATES	$59-139
	Reservation/cancellation policy
	2-night minimum stay on weekends
CREDIT CARDS	American Express, MasterCard, Visa
BREAKFAST	Continental plus, served in dining room
AMENITIES	Courtyard spa; all rooms w/queen or king beds, cable TV/radio & phones, suites have fireplaces; complimentary evening wine & hors d'oeuvres; off-street parking; FAX & 24-hr. telephone service w/modem hookups available
RESTRICTIONS	None. Resident Siamese cat, "Dizzy"

THE CHESHIRE CAT INN
BED & BREAKFAST

36 W. Valerio St.   Santa Barbara, CA 93101   (805) 569-1610
Christine Dunstan, Resident Owner   FAX: 805-682-1876
Margaret Goeden, Manager

LOCATION	Exit Hwy. 101 at Mission St., east for 5 blocks to State St., right for 3 blocks to Valerio, right to end of block
OPEN	All Year
DESCRIPTION	Two 1890 2-story Queen Anne Victorians & Coach House Antique, & country furnishings & Laura Ashley fabrics
NO. OF ROOMS	14 w/private baths
RATES	$75-249 Reservation/cancellation policy 2-night minimum on weekends
CREDIT CARDS	MasterCard, Visa
BREAKFAST	Full gourmet, served in dining room or on patio
AMENITIES	Hot tub in garden gazebo; all rooms w/robes, phones, fresh flowers, chocolates & liqueurs; fireplaces & TV/radio in common rooms; complimentary Saturday evening wine & cheese; bicycles available; meeting facilities
RESTRICTIONS	No smoking. No pets (resident dog, "Winnie", & cat, "Sidd"). Inquire about children
REVIEWED	*American Historic Bed & Breakfast Inns & Guesthouses* *America's Wonderful Little Hotels & Inns* *Bed & Breakfast in California* *Bed & Breakfast: Southern California* *Best Bed & Breakfasts & Country Inns: West* *California Country Inns & Itineraries* *Complete Guide to Bed & Breakfasts, Inns & Guesthouses* *Country Inns & Back Roads: California* *Inn Places for Bed & Breakfast* *Non-Smoker's Guide to Bed & Breakfast*
RATED	AAA 3 Diamonds

THE COTTAGE

840 Mission Canyon Rd.   Santa Barbara, CA 93105   *(805) 682-4461*
Ray & Sylvia Byers, Resident Owner

LOCATION	Just off of Foothills Rd. near the Old Mission, northeast of town. Map will be provided
OPEN	All Year (Closed Thanksgiving & Christmas)
DESCRIPTION	1954 Ranch Eclectic furnishings
NO. OF ROOMS	1-bedroom suite w/private bath, sitting room & refrigerator in private wing of main house (2nd bedroom available to same party)
RATES	Sgl/$65 Dbl/$75 $15 charge per extra person Inquire about 2nd night discount Reservation/cancellation policy 2-night minimum stay
CREDIT CARDS	No
BREAKFAST	Continental plus, provided in suite
AMENITIES	TV/radio in suite; outside entrance; complimentary fresh fruit
RESTRICTIONS	No smoking. No pets (resident dogs & cat). Inquire about children
REVIEWED	*Bed & Breakfast Homes Directory: West Coast* *Bed & Breakfast in California*
RSO	B&B of Los Angeles

EAGLE INN

232 Natoma Ave.   Santa Barbara, CA 93101   *(805) 965-3586*
Alan & Janet Bullock, Resident Owners

LOCATION	Near Pier & Marina, 1 block from West Beach
OPEN	All Year
DESCRIPTION	1931 Spanish Colonial Contemporary furnishings
NO. OF ROOMS	17 w/private baths
RATES	$85-110 Reservation/cancellation policy, 2-night minimum on weekends
CREDIT CARDS	All major cards
BREAKFAST	Continental, served in lobby
AMENITIES	TV/radio & phones in rooms
RESTRICTIONS	Smoking limited. No pets (resident cat)
RATED	AAA 2 Diamonds

THE FRANCISCAN INN

109 Bath St.   Santa Barbara, CA 93101   *(805) 963-8845*
Debbie Neer, Manager   *FAX: (805) 564-3295*

LOCATION	One block from beach, at corner of Bath St. & Mason St. Exit Hwy. 101 at Castillo if south bound, or Cabrillo Blvd. if north bound
OPEN	All Year
DESCRIPTION	1920, 1945 & 1976 California Spanish buildings Eclectic furnishings
NO. OF ROOMS	53 w/private baths (Including some suites)
RATES	Sgl/$60-135 Dbl/$65-155 Reservation/cancellation policy
CREDIT CARDS	American Express, Diner's Club, En Route, MasterCard, Visa
BREAKFAST	Continental plus, served in breakfast area of lobby
AMENITIES	Swimming pool, hot tub; all rooms w/HBO cable TV/radio & phones, some w/sitting areas, wet bars, & fully equipped kitchenettes; 1 w/fireplace; complimentary morning newspaper, & local calls
RESTRICTIONS	No pets
RATED	AAA 3 Diamonds Mobil 2 Stars

GLENBOROUGH INN

1327 Bath St.   Santa Barbara, CA 93101   (805) 966-0589
Michael Diaz, Resident Owner   FAX: (805) 564-2369

LOCATION	Exit Hwy. 101 at Carrillo, east 2 blocks to Bath, left 4 blocks to Inn
OPEN	All Year
DESCRIPTION	3 Turn-of-the-Century California Craftsman Homes Eclectic furnishings
NO. OF ROOMS	5 w/private baths 6 share 3 baths
RATES	PB/$100-160 SB/$65-90 Reservation/cancellation policy, 2-night minimum stay on weekends
CREDIT CARDS	American Express, Diner's Club, Discover, MasterCard, Visa
BREAKFAST	Full gourmet, served in parlor, guestrooms or gardens Picnic basket lunches available
AMENITIES	Gardens w/hot tub, parlour, phone in all rooms, fireplaces in 3; complimentary evening hors d'oeuvres & bedtime refreshments;
RESTRICTIONS	No smoking. No pets. Inquire about children
MEMBER	Professional Assn. of Innkeepers International
RATED	AAA 2 Diamonds

THE IVANHOE INN

1406 Castillo St.   Santa Barbara, CA 93101   (800) 428-1787
Mary Robinson, Resident Owner   FAX: (805) 683-8598

LOCATION	Exit Hwy. 101 at Arrellaga St. or Mission St., east to Castillo, right to corner of Sula St.
OPEN	All Year
DESCRIPTION	1905 2-story Victorian Country Victorian furnishings
NO. OF ROOMS	2 suites w/private baths 2 suites w/shared bath Cottage w/private bath & kitchen
RATES	PB/$85-175 SB/$110 Reservation/cancellation policy
CREDIT CARDS	American Express, MasterCard, Visa
BREAKFAST	Continental plus, delivered to room in picnic basket
AMENITIES	TV in most suites, some w/kitchens, fireplaces & phones; complimentary wine & cheese on 1st night of stay; small meeting facilities
RESTRICTIONS	None

LONG'S SEA VIEW BED & BREAKFAST

317 Piedmont Rd.   Santa Barbara, CA 93105   (805) 687-2947
Laverne Long, Resident Owner

LOCATION	Exit Hwy. 101 at Las Positas St. (name changes to San Roque), east on San Reque to Foothill (Hwy. 192), left to Ontare, right to Piedmont to 2nd house on right
OPEN	All Year
DESCRIPTION	Ranch Home Eclectic furnishings
NO. OF ROOMS	1 w/private bath
RATES	$75-79 Reservation/cancellation policy Discount for multiple night stays
CREDIT CARDS	No
BREAKFAST	Full, served in ocean view dining room, or on ocean view patio w/view of Channel Islands
AMENITIES	TV/radio in room; complimentary wine on arrival
RESTRICTIONS	No smoking

OCEAN VIEW HOUSE

312 Salida del Sol   PO Box 20065   Santa Barbara, CA 93104
Carolyn Canfield, Resident Owner   (805) 966-6659

LOCATION	3 blocks from the ocean & the lighthouse. Map sent w/deposit receipt
OPEN	All Year
DESCRIPTION	1950's California Ranch Antique furnishings
NO. OF ROOMS	2-room suite w/private bath
RATES	Sgl/$55 Dbl/$60 Reservation/cancellation policy 2-night minimum stay
CREDIT CARDS	No
BREAKFAST	Continental plus, served on patio or in suite
AMENITIES	Robes, TV/radio & phone & refrigerator in suite; complimentary soft drinks, wine & snacks; private entrance
RESTRICTIONS	No smoking. Inquire about pets (resident dog & cat)

OLD YACHT CLUB INN

431 Corona del Mar Dr.   Santa Barbara, CA 93103   (805) 962-1277
       CA (800) 549-1676   USA (800) 676-1676   FAX: (805) 962-3989
Nancy Donaldson, Sandy Hunt & Lu Caruso, Resident Owners

LOCATION	1 block from East Beach. Exit Hwy. 101 at Cabrillo Blvd., west approx. 1 mi., past bird refuge, to Corona del Mar Dr., right to Inn
OPEN	All Year
DESCRIPTION	1912 California Craftsman & adjacent 1925 Hitchcock House Turn-of-Century furnishings
NO. OF ROOMS	9 w/private baths
RATES	$75-140 Reservation/cancellation policy 2-night minimum on weekends
CREDIT CARDS	American Express, Discover, MasterCard, Visa
BREAKFAST	Full gourmet, served in dining room Picnic baskets & 5-course Saturday evening dinner available
AMENITIES	All rooms w/fresh flowers, decanter of sherry & phones, some w/private entrances & TV, 1 w/private deck; complimentary evening social hour w/wine & beverages; fireplace & grand piano in common room; bicycles, beach towels & chairs available; meeting facilities available if whole house booked
RESTRICTIONS	No smoking. No pets (resident West Highland Terriers & Toy Poodle)
AWARDS	1992 Best Inns, *Bon Appetite Magazine*
REVIEWED	*American Historic Bed & Breakfast Inns & Guesthouses* *America's Wonderful Little Hotels & Inns* *Bed & Breakfast in California* *Bed & Breakfast: Southern California* *Best Places to Kiss in Southern California* *Best Places to Stay in California* *Complete Guide to Bed & Breakfasts, Inns & Guesthouses* *Country Inns & Back Roads: California* *Fodor's Bed & Breakfasts, Country Inns & Other Weekend Pleasures—* *The West Coast* *Recommended Country Inns: West Coast*
RSO	B&B 800
MEMBER	B&B Innkeepers of Southern California Professional Assn. of Innkeepers International Santa Barbara B&B Innkeepers Guild
RATED	AAA 2 Diamonds ABBA 2 Crowns Mobil 2 Stars

THE OLIVE HOUSE

1604 Olive St.   Santa Barbara, CA 93101
Lois Gregg, Resident Owner

(805) 962-4902
(800) 786-6422

LOCATION	In residential area near the Mission & downtown. On corner of Arrellaga & Olive (request brochure for specific directions)
OPEN	All Year
DESCRIPTION	1904 2-story California Craftsman Eclectic furnishings
NO. OF ROOMS	6 w/private baths
RATES	Sgl/$100-155 Dbl/$105-155 Reservation/cancellation policy 2-night minimum stay on weekends
CREDIT CARDS	MasterCard, Visa
BREAKFAST	Continental plus, served in dining room
AMENITIES	Common room w/fireplace & grand piano; queen & king beds; all rooms w/radios & phones available, 1 w/TV & fireplace; complimentary afternoon & evening refreshments; meeting facilities; off-street parking
RESTRICTIONS	No smoking. No pets
REVIEWED	*American Historic Bed & Breakfast Inns & Guesthouses* *Bed & Breakfast in California* *Bed & Breakfast: Southern California* *Complete Guide to Bed & Breakfasts, Inns & Guesthouses*
MEMBER	Santa Barbara B&B Innkeepers Guild
RATED	AAA 2 Diamonds

THE PARSONAGE BED & BREAKFAST INN

1600 Olive St.   Santa Barbara, CA 93101
Dick & Audrey Harmon, Resident Innkeepers
Terry & Holli Harmon, Owners

(805) 962-9336
(800) 775-0352

LOCATION	Between downtown & the foothills, in the Upper East residential area. Exit Hwy. 101 at Mission St., east to Laguna St., right to Arrellaga St., left to Inn
OPEN	All Year
DESCRIPTION	1892 2-story Queen Anne Victorian Period furnishings National Historic Register
NO. OF ROOMS	6 w/private baths
RATES	$65-185 Reservation/cancellation policy 2-night minimum on weekends Inquire about off-season midweek discounts & weekly rates
CREDIT CARDS	American Express, MasterCard, Visa
BREAKFAST	Full, served fireside in formal dining room or on sundeck
AMENITIES	King or queen bed, robes & phones in rooms; fireplaces in living room & dining room; sundeck; complimentary afternoon refreshments; meeting facilities
RESTRICTIONS	No smoking. No pets. Children over 10

REVIEWED	*American Historic Bed & Breakfast Inns & Guesthouses*
	Bed & Breakfast in California
	Bed & Breakfast: Southern California
	Complete Guide to Bed & Breakfasts, Inns & Guesthouses
	Fodor's Bed & Breakfasts, Country Inns & Other Weekend Pleasures—
	    The West Coast
	The National Trust Guide to Historic Bed & Breakfasts, Inns &
	    Small Hotels

MEMBER	B&B in Southern California Santa Barbara Bed & Breakfast Innkeepers Guild
RATED	AAA 2 Diamonds

SIMPSON HOUSE INN

121 E. Arrellaga   Santa Barbara, CA 93101
Gillean Wilson, Manager

(800) 676-1280
FAX: (805) 564-4811

LOCATION	South Bound: Exit Hwy. 101 at Mission St. exit, left 6 blocks to Anacapa St., right 5 blocks to Arrellaga St., left 1/2 block to Inn North Bound: Exit Hwy. 101 at Arrellaga St. exit, 6-1/2 blocks to Inn
OPEN	All Year
DESCRIPTION	1874 2-story Eastlake Victorian with 2 wraparound verandas Antique furnishings Landmarks Commission Register
NO. OF ROOMS	6 rooms, 4 suites, & 3 cottages w/private baths
RATES	$75-225 Reservation/cancellation policy 2-night minimum stay on weekends Inquire about mid-week discount
CREDIT CARDS	American Express, Discover, MasterCard, Visa
BREAKFAST	Full gourmet, served in dining room, on private deck, garden veranda, patios, or in guestrooms
AMENITIES	English gardens; fireplaces & king or queen beds in suites & cottages; all rooms w/robes, TV/radio, phones, down comforters, fresh flowers, most w/king or queen beds; jacuzzi tubs in cottages; complimentary beverages & evening wine & hors d'oeuvres; bicycles, croquet, & beach equipment available; small meeting facilities; handicapped access
RESTRICTIONS	No smoking. No pets
AWARDS	Structure of Merit Award, 1985
REVIEWED	*American Historic Bed & Breakfast Inns & Guesthouses* *America's Wonderful Little Hotels & Inns* *Bed & Breakfast: California: A Select Guide* *Bed & Breakfast in California* *Bed & Breakfast: Southern California* *Best Places to Stay in California* *California Country Inns & Itineraries* *Country Inns & Back Roads: California* *Fodor's Bed & Breakfasts, Country Inns & Other Weekend Pleasures— The West Coast* *The National Trust Guide to Historic Bed & Breakfasts, Inns & Small Hotels*
MEMBER	Bed & Breakfast in Southern California California Assn. of B&B Inns Professional Assn. of Innkeepers International Santa Barbara B&B Innkeepers Guild
RATED	AAA 3 Diamonds ABBA 3 Crowns Mobil 3 Stars

TIFFANY INN

1323 De la Vina   Santa Barbara, CA 93101   (805) 963-2283
Carol MacDonald, Resident Owner   (800) 999-5672

LOCATION	North Bound: Exit Hwy. 101 at Arrellaga, left 3 blocks to De la Vina, right 2 blocks South Bound: Exit Hwy. 101 at Mission, left 3 blocks to De la Vina, right 7 blocks
OPEN	All Year
DESCRIPTION	1898 2-story Colonial Revival Victorian antique furnishings, & Laura Ashley prints
NO. OF ROOMS	3 w/private baths 2 w/shared bath 2 suites w/private baths
RATES	PB/$135 SB/$75 Suites/$175 Reservation/cancellation policy
CREDIT CARDS	American Express, MasterCard, Visa
BREAKFAST	Full, served in dining room or garden veranda
AMENITIES	All rooms w/queen beds, some w/fireplaces, TV/radios, garden or mountain views; 1 suite w/private entrance, jacuzzi tub, 1 w/private balcony, patio, jacuzzi tub w/view; complimentary afternoon & evening refreshments
RESTRICTIONS	No smoking. No pets
REVIEWED	*American Historic Bed & Breakfast Inns & Guesthouses* *Bed & Breakfast in California* *Bed & Breakfast: Southern California* *Best Places to Kiss in Southern California* *California Country Inns & Itineraries* *Complete Guide to Bed & Breakfasts, Inns & Guesthouses* *Country Inns & Backs Roads: California* *Recommended Country Inns: West Coas*
MEMBER	B&B Innkeepers of Southern California Professional Assn. of Innkeepers International Santa Barbara B&B Innkeepers Guild
RATED	AAA 3 Diamonds Mobil 2 Stars

THE UPHAM HOTEL
& GARDEN COTTAGES

1404 De la Vina St.   Santa Barbara, CA 93101   *(805) 962-0058*
Jan Martin Winn, Manager   *(800) 727-0876   FAX: (805) 963-2825*

LOCATION	Exit Hwy. 101 north at Arrellaga St., right 2 blocks to De la Vina, right 2 blocks. Hotel is on the left
OPEN	All Year
DESCRIPTION	1871 2-story Victorian w/carriage house, 5 garden cottages & restaurant Antique & period furnishing National Historic Register
NO. OF ROOMS	49 w/private baths
RATES	$95-165 Reservation/cancellation policy 2-night minimum stay on weekends
CREDIT CARDS	American Express, Diner's Club, Discover, MasterCard, Visa
BREAKFAST	Continental plus, served in lobby or on garden veranda Lunch & dinner available in restaurant
AMENITIES	All rooms w/TV/radio & phones, 8 w/fireplaces, master suite w/robes, jacuzzi tub, wet bar & private yard w/hammock; complimentary morning paper, afternoon wine & cheese, & cookies & coffee after dinner; banquet & conference facilities; FAX & same-day valet laundry & dry-cleaning services available
RESTRICTIONS	No pets (resident cat, "Bob")
AWARDS	Best Small Hotel, *San Francisco Focus*
REVIEWED	*American Historic Bed & Breakfast Inns & Guesthouses* *Annual Directory of American Bed & Breakfast* *Bed & Breakfast in California* *Best Places to Stay in California* *Complete Guide to Bed & Breakfasts, Inns & Guesthouses* *The National Trust Guide to Historic Bed & Breakfasts, Inns & Small Hotels*
RATED	AAA 2 Diamonds Mobil 2 Stars

VILLA ROSA INN

15 Chapala St. Santa Barbara, CA 93101   *(805) 966-0851*
Annie Puetz, General Manager   *FAX: (805) 962-7159*

LOCATION	On the beach just off Cabrillo Blvd. Map sent on request
OPEN	All Year
DESCRIPTION	1931 2-story Southwestern Villa Santa Fe Southwestern furnishings
NO. OF ROOMS	18 w/private baths
RATES	Summer—$90-190 Winter—$80-190 Inquire about corporate guest plan
CREDIT CARDS	American Express, MasterCard, Visa
BREAKFAST	Continental, served in guestroom, lobby or courtyard
AMENITIES	Garden courtyard w/swimming pool, jacuzzi; all rooms w/TV/radio, phones, king or queen beds, deluxe rooms have fireplaces; complimentary morning paper, evening wine & hors d'oeuvres, & bedtime sherry; masseuse, dry cleaning & room service available; meeting facilities; guest privileges at Santa Barbara Athletic Club
RESTRICTIONS	No pets. Children over 14
AWARDS	INNovations Top Ten B&Bs of the Year, 1991 & 1992
REVIEWED	*American Historic Bed & Breakfast Inns & Guesthouses* *America's Wonderful Little Hotels & Inns* *Best Places to Stay in California* *Bed & Breakfast in California* *Bed & Breakfast: Southern California* *California Country Inns & Itineraries* *Complete Guide to Bed & Breakfasts, Inns & Guesthouses* *Country Inns & Back Roads: California* *Fodor's Bed & Breakfast Guide* *Inn Places for Bed & Breakfast in the West*
RATED	AAA 2 Diamonds

SANTA CATALINA ISLAND
(AVALON & TWO HARBORS)

This dreamlike island paradise with Mediterranean overtones, 26 miles off the mainland, is hard to leave. William Wrigley once owned most of it, and now the Catalina Conservancy owns and protects 86% of it as an open wilderness. Choose Avalon's car-free resort atmosphere, or trek into the pristine and rugged interior and look for wildlife — bison, wild pigs, goats, deer and tiny island foxes. Some local events include marathon and 10-K races in January and March, Chamber Music Festival in June and the U.S. Championship Outrigger race in August. Get there by ferry, helicopter or hydrofoil from Long Beach, San Pedro, or Newport Beach.

BANNING HOUSE LODGE

PO Box 5044   Two Harbors, CA 90704-5044   (310) 510-2800
Marianne Whittington, Manager   FAX: (310) 510-1354

LOCATION	Take Catalina Express boat from San Pedro to Two Harbors. Hostess will meet guests at boat
OPEN	All Year
DESCRIPTION	1910 2-story Craftsman Eclectic furnishings
NO. OF ROOMS	11 w/private baths
RATES	Summer/$105-180 Winter/$54.60-140
CREDIT CARDS	MasterCard, Visa
BREAKFAST	Continental, served in dining room Dinner available
RESTRICTIONS	No pets (resident cat). Inquire about children
REVIEWED	*Bed & Breakfast: Southern California*

CATALINA ISLAND INN

125 Metropole Ave. PO Box 467 Avalon, CA 90704   (310) 510-1623
Martin & Bernardine Curtin, Resident Owners   FAX: (310) 510-7218

LOCATION	Once on the Island, take Crescent to Metropole
OPEN	All Year
DESCRIPTION	1906 San Francisco Victorian Contemporary rattan furnishings
NO. OF ROOMS	36 w/private baths
RATES	Sgl/$45-95 Dbl/$95-160 Reservation/cancellation policy 2-night minimum June 15-October 1
CREDIT CARDS	American Express, Discover, MasterCard, Visa
BREAKFAST	Continental, served in lobby area
AMENITIES	TV/radio in rooms; ceiling fans; window shutters
RESTRICTIONS	No pets

GARDEN HOUSE INN

125 Clarissa St. PO Box 1881 Avalon, CA 90704   (310) 510-0356
Jon & Cathy Olsen, Resident Owners

LOCATION	Just off Crescent Ave., on corner of 3rd & Clarissa
OPEN	All Year
DESCRIPTION	1923 3-story Townhouse Elegant small hotel with Country French furnishings
NO. OF ROOMS	9 w/private baths
RATES	$125-250 Reservation/cancellation policy, 2-night minimum on weekends
CREDIT CARDS	American Express, MasterCard, Visa
BREAKFAST	Continental plus buffet, served in living room or courtyard
AMENITIES	Garden courtyard, ocean view sundeck; living room w/fireplace; all rooms w/TV/VCR/radio & queen sized beds
RESTRICTIONS	No smoking. No pets
RATED	AAA 3 Diamonds

GULL HOUSE BED & BREAKFAST

344 Whittley Ave.   PO Box 1381   Avalon, CA 90704
Bob & Hattie Michalis, Resident Owners

(310) 510-2547
FAX: (310) 510-7606

LOCATION	Close to center of town
OPEN	April 1-October 30
DESCRIPTION	1981 2-story Contemporary Contemporary furnishings
NO. OF ROOMS	2 suites w/private baths 2 rooms w/private baths
RATES	Suites/$135-145 Room/$110-125 Reservation/cancellation policy 2-night minimum stay 5% Senior discount
CREDIT CARDS	No
BREAKFAST	Continental plus, served on patio
AMENITIES	Patio w/swimming pool, sauna & barbeque; suites w/fireplaces, sitting room & refrigerator; TV/radio/CD in all rooms; small meeting facilities; complimentary taxi passes with advance payment
RESTRICTIONS	No smoking. No pets
REVIEWED	*Bed & Breakfast in California* *Bed & Breakfast: Southern California* *Complete Guide to Bed & Breakfasts, Inns & Guesthouses*
MEMBER	American B&B Assn.
RATED	AAA 3 Diamonds

THE INN ON MT. ADA

398 Wrigley Rd.   PO Box 2560   Avalon, CA 90704   *(310) 510-2030*
Marlewe McAdam & Susie Griffin, Resident Owners   *FAX: (310) 510-2337*

LOCATION	On Mt. Ada, overlooking the ocean. Van will provide transportation from boat terminal & heliport
OPEN	All Year
DESCRIPTION	1921 Georgian Colonial Former Wrigley Mansion Traditional elegant furnishings on 5-1/2 acres National Historic Register
NO. OF ROOMS	4 w/private baths 2 suites w/private baths & sitting ooms
RATES	Rooms/$230-490 Suites/$370-590 Reservation/cancellation policy 2-night minimum stay on weekends
CREDIT CARDS	MasterCard, Visa
BREAKFAST	Full, served in ocean-view dining room Lunch & dinner included in rate
AMENITIES	Robes, & TV/radio in all rooms, some w/fireplaces; complimentary early bird coffee, afternoon wine & hors d'oeuvres, fruit & cookies, & use of golf carts; meeting facilities
RESTRICTIONS	No smoking. No pets (resident pet in owners quarters). Children over 14
REVIEWED	*Bed & Breakfast in California* *Best Places to Stay in California* *California Country Inns & Itineraries* *Country Inns & Back Roads: California* *The National Trust Guide to Historic Bed & Breakfasts, Inns &* *Small Hotels*
MEMBER	Professional Assn. of Innkeepers International
RATED	Mobil 4 Stars

THE OLD TURNER INN
BED & BREAKFAST

232 Catalina Ave.   PO Box 97   Avalon, CA 90704   *(310) 510-2236*
Jeanne Hill, Owner   Joyce McArthy, Manager

LOCATION	One block from Green Pleasure Pier
OPEN	All Year
DESCRIPTION	1927 2-story Cape Cod Country furnishings
NO. OF ROOMS	5 w/private baths
RATES	$110-175 Reservation/cancellation policy, 2-night minimum on weekends
CREDIT CARDS	Discover, MasterCard, Visa
BREAKFAST	Continental plus, served in living room
AMENITIES	Fireplaces in 4 rooms & living room; sunporches; ceiling fans; TV/radio in rooms; complimentary wine, soft drinks & appetizers
RESTRICTIONS	No smoking. No pets (resident cat). Inquire about children

ZANE GREY PUEBLO HOTEL

199 Chimes Tower Rd.   PO Box 216   Avalon, CA 90704   *(310) 510-0966*
Kevin Anderson, Manager   *(310) 510-1520*

LOCATION	At top of Chimes Tower Rd., within walking distance of town
OPEN	All Year
DESCRIPTION	1926 Hopi-style multi-building Pueblo. Built by Zane Grey Southwestern furnishings
NO. OF ROOMS	18 w/private baths
RATES	$55-110 Reservation/cancellation policy 2-night minimum stay on summer weekends
CREDIT CARDS	American Express, MasterCard, Visa
BREAKFAST	Continental, served on patio
AMENITIES	Fresh-water swimming pool, 2 sundecks; all rooms w/queen beds; living room w/fireplace & grand piano; courtesy taxi service; meeting facilities
RESTRICTIONS	No pets (resident cat). Children 10 & over

SANTA MONICA

This trendy city with its broad, white beaches, promenade, restored historic pier and upscale homes is becoming a major resort area. It's also the gateway to the Santa Monica Mountains National Recreation Area, a 50-mile stretch (of 150,000 acres) considered a "botanical island." On Pacific Coast Highway, west of Los Angeles via I-10.

CHANNEL ROAD INN

219 W. Channel Rd.   Santa Monica, CA 90402   *(310) 459-1920*
Susan Zolla & Kathy Jensen, Resident Owners   *FAX: (310) 454-9920*

LOCATION	In Santa Monica Canyon, 1 block from beach
OPEN	All Year
DESCRIPTION	1910 3-story Colonial Revival Antique & eclectic furnishings
NO. OF ROOMS	14 w/private baths
RATES	$85-195 Reservation/cancellation policy
CREDIT CARDS	MasterCard, Visa
BREAKFAST	Full, served in breakfast room, library, guestrooms, or on patio
AMENITIES	Hillside hot tub overlooking Santa Monica Bay; library; fireplace in living room; robes, cable TV/radio, phones & fresh flowers in rooms; complimentary afternoon tea, wine & hors d'oeuvres; small meeting facilities; limited handicapped access; complimentary use of bicycle
RESTRICTIONS	No smoking. No pets
AWARDS	Grand Hotel Award 1992, *San Francisco Focus* Renovation of the Year, 1990
REVIEWED	*America's Wonderful Little Hotels & Inns* *Bed & Breakfast: Southern California* *Bed & Breakfast U.S.A.* *Best Places to Kiss in Southern California* *California Country Inns & Itineraries* *Country Inns & Back Roads: California* *Fodor's Bed & Breakfasts, Country Inns & Other Weekend Pleasures— The West Coast* *Official Guide to American Historic Bed & Breakfast Inns & Guesthouses*
MEMBER	California Assn. of B&B Inns
RATED	AAA 3 Diamonds Mobil 3 Stars

WOERNER'S GUEST HOUSE

(RSO)   *Reservations: (415) 696-1690   FAX: (415) 696-1699*

LOCATION	At Pacific & 4th
OPEN	All Year
DESCRIPTION	1970s Contemporary Contemporary furnishings
NO. OF ROOMS	1 w/private bath
RATES	$75 Reservation/cancellation policy 2-night minimum stay
CREDIT CARDS	MasterCard, Visa
BREAKFAST	Continental plus, served on deck or in guesthouse
AMENITIES	TV/radio & phone in room
RESTRICTIONS	No smoking. No pets
RSO	B&B International

SANTA PAULA
(VENTURA)

Two claims to fame here: the Citrus Capital of the World and the Antique Airplane Capital of the World. Take the walking tour and don't miss the Unocal Oil Museum, the Santa Paula Theater, the General Store and the Mill. Twelve miles east of Ventura on Hwy. 126.

THE FERN OAKS INN

1025 Ojai Rd.   Santa Paula, CA 93060
Gil & Cheryl Eigenhuis, Resident Owners

(805) 525-7747
FAX: (805) 933-5001

LOCATION	Hwy. 126 east to 10th St. Exit., 1 mi. to Santa Paula St., right on Ojai Rd. Inn is on the right at corner of Fern Oaks Rd.
OPEN	All Year
DESCRIPTION	1929 2-story Spanish Revival Elegant eclectic furnishings On 3/4 acre
NO. OF ROOMS	4 w/private baths
RATES	$80-110 Reservation/cancellation policy 2-night minimum during holidays
CREDIT CARDS	For reservation guarantee only
BREAKFAST	Full gourmet, served in formal dining room, sun porch or pool deck Special dinners available by arrangement
AMENITIES	Heated swimming pool; solarium; fireplace in common area; all rooms w/queen beds, separate vanity areas, & radio w/cassette players; complimentary wine, beverages, & cookies; in-room massage available w/1 week advance notice
RESTRICTIONS	No smoking. No pets (resident Pomeranian, alley cat, Canaries, Cockateel & Cockatoo)
REVIEWED	*Bed & Breakfast: Southern California* *The West Coast Bed & Breakfast Guide: California, Oregon &* *Washington*
RSO	B&B of Southern California

THE WHITE GABLES INN

715 E. Santa Paula St.   Santa Paula, CA 93060   *(805) 933-3041*
Bob & Ellen Smith, Resident Owners

LOCATION	In Historic District. Exit Hwy. 126 at 10th St., to northwest corner of Santa Paula & Walnut St.
OPEN	All Year
DESCRIPTION	1894 3-story Queen Anne Victorian Antique furnishings County of Ventura Heritage Landmark
NO. OF ROOMS	2 w/private baths 1 suite w/private bath & sitting room
RATES	Rooms/$85-95 Suite/$115 Reservation/cancellation policy Inquire about mid-week & winter rates
CREDIT CARDS	MasterCard, Visa
BREAKFAST	Full, served in formal dining room
AMENITIES	All rooms w/radios & candy, 1 w/terrycloth robes & 1 w/private porch; phone available; piano in parlor; complimentary sherry; small meeting facilities, off-street parking
RESTRICTIONS	No smoking. No pets (resident cats in owners' quarters).No children
REVIEWED	*Bed & Breakfast: Southern California*
MEMBER	Professional Assn. of Innkeepers International

SEAL BEACH
(LONG BEACH)

A surprisingly nice little beach town just across the bay from Long Beach, and handy to all the sights. On a thumb-shaped peninsula next to the U.S. Naval Weapons Station and the must-see Seal Beach National Wildlife Refuge.

THE SEAL BEACH INN & GARDENS

212 Fifth St.   Seal Beach, CA 90740
Marjorie Bettenhausen, Owner
Wendy Stewart, Resident Manager

(310) 493-2416   (800) 443-3292
FAX: (310) 799-0483

LOCATION	1 block from beach. From Pacific Coast Hwy., take 5th St. 3 blocks to corner of 5th & Central
OPEN	All Year
DESCRIPTION	1923 Restored 2-story French Mediterranean Antique furnishings
NO. OF ROOMS	23 w/private baths (Including cottages & suites)
RATES	$108-175 Reservation/cancellation policy Mid-week corporate rates
CREDIT CARDS	American Express, Diner's Club, Discover, MasterCard, Visa
BREAKFAST	Full, served in dining room Lunch, dinner & special meals available by advance notice
AMENITIES	Swimming pool; lush gardens w/antique statuary; courtyard & fountains; complimentary afternoon refreshments w/wine & cheese; whirlpool tub in 1 room; fireplace in 1 room & library; kitchens in some cottages & suites; TV/radio, phones & cookies in all rooms; meeting facilities; limited handicapped access
RESTRICTIONS	No smoking. No pets. Inquire about children
RSO	B&B 800
MEMBER	American B&B Assn. American Hotel/Motel Assn. California Assn. of B&B Inns California Hotel/Motel Assn. International Innkeepers Assn.
RATED	AAA 2 Diamonds ABBA 3 Crowns Mobil 3 Stars

SEQUOIA NATIONAL FOREST

In the center of the magnificent Sequoia National Forest, home of the giant sequoia and the Wild and Scenic Kern River. Look for spotted owls and fall colors around Quaking Aspen Road and Road's End. Just north of Lake Isabella. From Bakersfield, 55 miles northeast via Hwys 99, 178 and 155.

ROAD'S END AT POSO CREEK

Mailing address: RR 1, Box 450   Posey, CA 93260   (805) 536-8668
Jane Baxter, Resident Owner

LOCATION	In Poso Park Community, 55 mi. northeast of Bakersfield, and directly north of Kernville, in Sequoia National Forest (map provided)
OPEN	All Year
DESCRIPTION	1919 2-story California Cottage Antique furnishings
NO. OF ROOMS	2 w/1-1/2 baths & enclosed open-air outdoor shower (accommodates 4)
RATES	$75-95 Reservation/cancellation policy 2-night minimum on weekends
CREDIT CARDS	No
BREAKFAST	Full, served in dining room, gardens, on tree house deck, or creekside Lunch & dinner available by advance request
AMENITIES	Hot tub & deck; robes & phones in rooms; fireplace & TV/radio in living room; garden hammocks; complimentary afternoon wine & hors d'oeuvres; meeting facilities; limited handicapped access
RESTRICTIONS	No smoking. No pets (resident cat, "Archie"). Inquire about children
REVIEWED	*Bed & Breakfast Homes Directory: West Coast* *Bed & Breakfast: Southern California* *Bed & Breakfast U.S.A.*
MEMBER	Sequoia Region Tourism Council

SKYFOREST
(LAKE ARROWHEAD)

A good place to stay while enjoying all the benefits of Lake Arrowhead resort. Santa's Village is here, too, right on the Scenic Rim of the World Drive.

SKYFOREST BED & BREAKFAST INN

760 Kuffel Canyon Rd.   PO Box 482   Skyforest, CA 92385
Meta & Tom Morgan, Resident Managers   *(909) 337-4680*

LOCATION	Center of town on the right side of Hwy. 18
OPEN	All Year
DESCRIPTION	1986 2-story wood & glass Mountain Chalet Contemporary country furnishings
NO. OF ROOMS	2 w/private baths 2 w/shared bath
RATES	PB/$100-150 SB/$75-90 Reservation/cancellation policy 2-night minimum on weekends Inquire about ski packages January-March
CREDIT CARDS	No
BREAKFAST	Weekends/Full Weekdays/Continental Served in dining room or breakfast room
AMENITIES	Fireplaces in common rooms; jacuzzi tub in master suite; private & semi-private decks; complimentary afternoon wine & hors d'oeuvres on weekends
RESTRICTIONS	No smoking. No pets (resident cat in manager's quarters). No children. Snow chains may be needed November-March
REVIEWED	*Bed & Breakfast: Southern California*

STORYBOOK INN

28717 Hwy. 18   PO Box 362   Skyforest, CA 92385   (909) 336-1483
Kathleen & John Wooley, Resident Owners   (800) 554-9208

LOCATION	On Hwy. 18, 1 mi. east of Hwy 173, & just east of Skyforest & Kuffel Canyon
OPEN	All Year
DESCRIPTION	1942 3-story Swiss Chalet Country & antique furnishings
NO. OF ROOMS	9 rooms & suites w/private baths 2-bedroom cabin w/2 baths, fireplace, sleeping loft & kitchen
RATES	Rooms & Suites/$98-165 Cabin/$200 Reservation/cancellation policy 2-night minimum on weekends 3-night minimum during holidays Midweek & senior discounts
CREDIT CARDS	No
BREAKFAST	Continental plus, served in dining room or guestroom
AMENITIES	Hot tub in glass-enclosed Oriental garden w/pagoda fireplaces in lobby/study; all rooms w/fresh flowers, TV/radio, some suites w/glass-enclosed solariums or porches; complimentary morning paper, evening wine & hors d'oeuvres & bedtime cookies, conference room
RESTRICTIONS	No smoking. No pets
REVIEWED	*American Historic Bed & Breakfast Inns & Guesthouses* *America's Wonderful Little Hotels & Inns* *Bed & Breakfast in California* *Bed & Breakfast: Southern California* *Complete Guide to American Bed & Breakfast* *Complete Guide to Bed & Breakfasts, Inns & Guesthouses* *The Non-Smokers' Guide to Bed & Breakfast*
RSO	B&B 800
MEMBER	B&B Innkeepers of Southern California

SOLVANG

A little bit of Denmark in the beautiful Santa Ynez Valley, founded by Danes in 1911. Windmills mark the spot, and the pastries are to die for. Tour the town via "Honen," horse-drawn streetcars. Danish Days in September is a major event, as are the summerlong performances at the acclaimed Theaterfest, held in a 780-seat outdoor Festival Theater. From Santa Barbara, 45 miles northwest via Hwy. 101. On the way, stop off at Gaviota Beach State Park.

HOMESTAY

(RSO)   *Reservations: (805) 544-4406   FAX: (805) 546-8642*

LOCATION	Inquire
OPEN	All Year
DESCRIPTION	Contemporary Home Eclectic furnishings
NO. OF ROOMS	1 w/private bath
RATES	$50-60 Reservation/cancellation policy Minimum stay during holiday weekends
CREDIT CARDS	No
BREAKFAST	Full, served in dining area
AMENITIES	Complimentary snacks & beverages
RESTRICTIONS	No smoking. No pets. No children
RSO	Megan's Friends B&B Reservation Service

PETERSEN VILLAGE INN

1576 Mission Dr. Solvang, CA 93463   (805) 688-3121 CA   (800) 321-8985
Earl & Dolores Petersen, Resident Owner   FAX: *(805) 688-5732*

LOCATION	In Petersen Village, town center
OPEN	All Year
DESCRIPTION	1976 2-story Danish Danish antiques & European furnishings
NO. OF ROOMS	40 suites w/private baths
RATES	$95-165 Reservation/cancellation policy 2-night minimum stay on weekends
CREDIT CARDS	American Express, MasterCard, Visa
BREAKFAST	European continental buffet, served in Courtyard Cafe
AMENITIES	Complimentary evening wine hour w/entertainment, piano & coffee/tea room service; canopied beds & TV/phones in rooms, tower suite w/fireplace & private conference room w/bar
RESTRICTIONS	No pets
REVIEWED	*Bed & Breakfast in California* *Country Inns & Back Roads: California* *Elegant Small Hotels: A Connoisseur's Guide*
MEMBER	The Innkeepers' Register
RATED	AAA 4 Diamonds Mobil 3 Stars

SPRINGVILLE

The Sequoia National Forest is at the front door of this northwestern gateway into the groves. Remember this is the National Forest, not the National Park. Handy to Lake Success and just above the Tule River Indian Reservation. About 30 miles southeast of Visalia.

ANNIE'S BED & BREAKFAST

33024 Globe Dr.   Springville, CA 93265   *(209) 539-3827*
John & Ann Bozanich, Resident Owners

LOCATION	14 mi. east of Porterville via Hwy 190, then right on Globe 1/4 mi.
OPEN	All Year
DESCRIPTION	Early 1900's Country Boarding House & Bunkhouse Antique furnishings On 5 acres
NO. OF ROOMS	3 w/private baths
RATES	$75-85 Reservation/cancellation policy $10 mid-week discount
CREDIT CARDS	American Express, Diner's Club, MasterCard, Visa
BREAKFAST	Full, served in dining room, guestroom, poolside, or on deck Catered dinner available, by advance notice, at extra charge
AMENITIES	Decks, swimming pool, hot tub; all rooms have private entrances, feather mattresses, handmade quilts, robes & phones, 2 open to the pool; afternoon or evening refreshments; meeting/wedding facilities
RESTRICTIONS	No smoking. No pets (resident critters: pet pig, "Blossom," horses, Pot Belly house pig, "Boo," 3 dogs, "Bozco," "Buster" & "Panda," & 20 cats). Children over 12
REVIEWED	*Bed & Breakfast: Southern California*

MOUNTAIN TOP BED & BREAKFAST

56816 Aspen Dr.   Springville, CA 93265   *(209) 542-2639*
Mailing address: 607 Ponderosa, Rt. 2   Springville, CA 93265
Claudia & Richard Ayotte, Resident Owners

LOCATION	In the mountains of the Sequoia National Forest, 34 mi. east of town on Hwy. 190 in the Ponderosa development
OPEN	All Year
DESCRIPTION	Mountain Pine Home at 7200 ft. Eclectic furnishings
NO. OF ROOMS	2 w/shared bath
RATES	$60 Reservation/cancellation policy
CREDIT CARDS	No
BREAKFAST	Continental, served in dining room Other meals available at Ponderosa Lodge
AMENITIES	TV/VCR & video tapes in rooms; complimentary bottle of champagne on arrival; fireplace in living room; meeting facilities
RESTRICTIONS	No smoking. No children. Resident dog & cat
REVIEWED	*Bed & Breakfast: Southern California* *Bed & Breakfast Homes Directory*

SUMMERLAND
(SANTA BARBARA)

Just down the road from Santa Barbara, this pleasant little town has a very private nude beach for skinny-dippers.

INN ON SUMMER HILL

2520 Lillie Ave.   PO Box 376   Summerland, CA 93067   (805) 969-9998
Verlinda Richardson, Manager   (800) 845-5566   FAX: (805) 969-9998

LOCATION	From Hwy. 101 Evans Ave. exit, go south on Lillie
OPEN	All Year
DESCRIPTION	1989 2-story California Craftsman English country furnishings
NO. OF ROOMS	16 w/private baths
RATES	Weekends/$185-275 Weekdays/$145-210 Reservation/cancellation policy 2-nights on weekends & holidays
CREDIT CARDS	American Express, MasterCard, Visa
BREAKFAST	Full, served in dining room or in bed
AMENITIES	Hot tub; all rooms w/ocean views, balconies or patios robes, fireplaces, TV/VCP/radio/cassette players, jacuzzi tubs, down comforters, canopy beds, fresh flowers, & hair dryers; complimentary afternoon refreshments & evening dessert; small meeting facilities; handicapped access
RESTRICTIONS	No smoking. No pets. Inquire about children
REVIEWED	*America's Wonderful Little Hotels & Inns* *Bed & Breakfast: Southern California* *Complete Guide to Bed & Breakfasts, Inns & Guesthouses* *Fodor's Bed & Breakfasts, Country Inns & Other Weekend Pleasures—* * The West Coast*
MEMBER	California Assn. of Bed & Breakfast Inns
RATED	AAA 4 Diamonds ABBA 4 Crowns Mobil 3 Stars

SUMMERLAND INN

2161 Ortega Hill Rd. PO Box 1209 Summerland, CA 93067
James R. Farned, Resident Owner
(805) 969-5225

LOCATION	From Hwy. 101 north, exit at Evans Ave., right to Ortega Hill Rd., turn left
	From Hwy. 101 south, exit at Summerland, left to Ortega Hill Rd., turn left
OPEN	All Year
DESCRIPTION	1986 2-story New England Colonial Country furnishings
NO. OF ROOMS	11 w/private baths
RATES	Weekends/$90-130 Weekdays/$55-90 Reservation/cancellation policy 2-night minimum stay on weekends
CREDIT CARDS	American Express, Diner's Club, Discover, MasterCard, Visa
BREAKFAST	Continental plus, served in guestrooms
AMENITIES	All rooms w/TV & phones, some have fireplaces & ocean views; fireplace in common area; complimentary sherry; handicapped access
RESTRICTIONS	No smoking. No pets. Children over 15
REVIEWED	*America's Wonderful Little Hotels & Inns* *Complete Guide to Bed & Breakfasts, Inns & Guesthouses*
RATED	AAA 3 Diamonds

SUNSET BEACH

Between Seal Beach and Huntington Beach you will find Sunset Beach with its shops, restaurants, marina and access to the wonders of Orange County.

HARBOUR INN

16912 Pacific Coast Hwy.   PO Box 1439
Sunset Beach, CA 90742
Mary Lamberton, Manager

(310) 592-4770
(714) 846-1765
FAX: (310) 592-3547

LOCATION	1 block from beach, at city limits
OPEN	All Year
DESCRIPTION	1989 2-story European Country Inn European Country furnishings
NO. OF ROOMS	23 w/private baths
RATES	Sgl/$59-109 Dbl/$69-119 Reservation/cancellation policy
CREDIT CARDS	American Express, Carte Blanche, Diner's Club, Discover; MasterCard, Visa
BREAKFAST	Continental plus, served in lounge
AMENITIES	Ocean & harbor views; cable TV & phones in rooms; complimentary beverages, & occasional wine & cheese; handicapped access; meeting/conference facilities
RESTRICTIONS	No pets. No parties
RATED	AAA 3 Diamonds

TEMECULA

Wine lovers alert: this center of the prime grape growing region of the Temecula Valley will delight and amaze. First, see the downtown's Old West Main Street, The Bank and the Old Town Museum. Then east of town begins a circular route to 13 wineries and vineyards — all offer tours and tastings. The major event: The annual Balloon and Wine Festival in May packs the town. There's great fishing and swimming at nearby Lake Skinner Recreation Area. And about 20 miles north, drop in at the Perris Valley Airport, one of the biggest jump centers in the world. Temecula is halfway between Riverside and San Diego on I-15.

LOMA VISTA BED & BREAKFAST

33350 La Serena Way   Temecula, CA 92591
Betty & Dick Ryan, Resident Owners

(909) 676-7047

LOCATION	Exit I-15 at Rancho California Rd., east 4-1/2 mi. to 1st dirt road on left past Callaway Winery
OPEN	All Year (Closed Thanksgiving, Christmas & New Year's)
DESCRIPTION	1987 2-story California Mission Style Eclectic furnishings
NO. OF ROOMS	6 w/private baths
RATES	$95-125 Reservation/cancellation policy
CREDIT CARDS	Discover, MasterCard, Visa
BREAKFAST	Full w/champagne, served in formal dining room
AMENITIES	Fireplace in living room; air conditioning & radios in rooms; complimentary beverages & cookies all day, & evening wine & cheese on the patio; small meeting facilities
RESTRICTIONS	No smoking. No pets (resident Dalmatian)
AWARDS	Top 10 Inns 1991, *INNovations*
REVIEWED	*America's Wonderful Little Hotels & Inns* *Bed & Breakfast American Style* *Bed & Breakfast in California* *Bed & Breakfast: Southern California* *Bed & Breakfast U.S.A.* *Best Places to Stay in California* *Complete Guide to Bed & Breakfasts, Inns & Guesthouses* *Country Inns of California* *Fodor's Bed & Breakfasts, Country Inns & Other Weekend Pleasures—* * The West Coast* *Frommer's San Diego* *Inn Places for Bed & Breakfast*
RSO	B&B 800
MEMBER	B&B Innkeepers of Southern California
RATED	AAA 3 Diamonds

TEMPLETON

The Old West still lives on Main St. in this rural community. At San Luis Obispo, jog onto Hwy. 101, head 20 miles north. The gorgeous, scenic drive through Santa Margarita and Atascadero is worth the trip. Very handy to fun doings in Paso Robles.

HOMESTAY

(RSO)   *Reservations: (805) 544-4406   FAX: (805) 546-8642*

LOCATION	Inquire
OPEN	All Year
DESCRIPTION	Contemporary Home w/cabin Eclectic furnishings
NO. OF ROOMS	Cabin w/private bath
RATES	$90 Reservation/cancellation policy Minimum stay during holiday weekends
CREDIT CARDS	No
BREAKFAST	Continental, provided in cabin
AMENITIES	Fireplace
RESTRICTIONS	No pets (resident cat & dog). No children
RSO	Megan's Friends B&B Reservation Service

THREE RIVERS
(KINGS CANYON)

The three forks of the Kaweah River join together here. What more perfect setting as the main gateway into Kings Canyon National Park and Giant Forest Village and the beginning of the spactacular General's Highway.

CORT COTTAGE

PO Box 245   Three Rivers, CA 93271   *(209) 561-4671*
Gary & Catherine Cort, Owners

LOCATION	Map sent w/reservation confirmation
OPEN	All Year
DESCRIPTION	1985 Contemporary Cottage Custom designed by owner Eclectic furnishings
NO. OF ROOMS	Guesthouse w/private bath, living room, bedroom, kitchen & private deck
RATES	$70-75 Reservation/cancellation policy 2-night minimum stay
CREDIT CARDS	No
BREAKFAST	Continental plus, provided in cottage
AMENITIES	Hot tub; robes; TV/radio; sunken bath tub; complimentary beverages
RESTRICTIONS	No smoking. No pets (resident cat at main house)
REVIEWED	*Bed & Breakfast Homes Directory: West Coast* *Bed & Breakfast in California* *Bed & Breakfast U.S.A.* *Complete Guide to Bed & Breakfasts, Inns & Guesthouses*
RSO	B&B International

TWENTYNINE PALMS

In the 1870s, 29 palms bordered this oasis between the Mojave and Colorado Deserts. Now it's the northern entrance into 870 square miles of Joshua Tree National Monument, and sits at the southern edge of the Marine Corps Air Ground Combat Center. Entrance is very restricted — opt for the joshuas. 43 miles northeast of Palm Springs on Hwy. 62.

29 PALMS INN

73950 Inn Ave.   Twentynine Palms, CA 92277
Jane Grunt-Smith, Resident Owner

(619) 367-3505
FAX: (619) 367-4425

LOCATION	From east Hwy. 62, go right on National Monument Dr., & right on Inn Ave.
OPEN	All Year
DESCRIPTION	1928-1960 Adobe Eclectic furnishings
NO. OF ROOMS	16 w/private baths
RATES	Sgl/$30-75 Dbl/$40-95 Reservation/cancellation policy 2-night minimum stay on holidays
CREDIT CARDS	American Express, MasterCard, Visa
BREAKFAST	Continental, served in common area Sunday brunch available
AMENITIES	Swimming pool, hot tub; fireplaces, TV/radios in rooms; complimentary coffee; small meeting facilities
RESTRICTIONS	No smoking. Inquire about pets (resident ducks, geese & other wildlife)
REVIEWED	*Hidden Los Angeles & Southern California*

VENICE

Filmakers love the beachfront community just south of Santa Monica and next to Marina del Rey, via Hwy. 1, but it still struggles with its image. Check out the amazing murals that adorn public buildings, and the wacky parade of the truly bizarre on the boardwalk. Fun, but be careful out there after dark.

VENICE BEACH HOUSE

15 30th Ave.   Venice, CA 90291   *(310) 823-1966   FAX: (310) 823-1842*
Betty Lou Weiner, Manager

LOCATION	Exit Hwy. 405 south at Washington Blvd., west to last street before beach, right 2-1/2 blocks to 29th Place, then right into parking lot
OPEN	All Year
DESCRIPTION	1911 2-story California Craftsman Period furnishings National Historic Register
NO. OF ROOMS	5 w/private baths 4 w/shared baths
RATES	PB/$110-150 SB/$80-90 Reservation/cancellation policy
CREDIT CARDS	American Express, MasterCard, Visa
BREAKFAST	Continental plus, served in breakfast room, guestroom, or on veranda Picnic baskets available
AMENITIES	Fireplace in 1 room; TV/radio & phones in all rooms; complimentary afternoon tea & evening refreshments; bicycles available
RESTRICTIONS	No smoking. No pets
REVIEWED	*American Historic Bed & Breakfast Inns & Guesthouses* *Bed & Breakfast in California* *Bed & Breakfast: Southern California* *Complete Guide to Bed & Breakfasts, Inns & Guesthouses* *Country Inns of the Far West: California* *Inn Places for Bed & Breakfast* *Recommended Country Inns: West Coast*

VENTURA

There are two good reasons to come here: the city's outstanding beaches, especially Point Mugu State Park, and it's a main access point to the Channel Islands, "America's Galapagos," 15 miles offshore. In town, tour Old San Buenaventura historic area. On Hwy. 101, 30 miles south of Santa Barbara, and just this side of the Los Angeles sprawl. Handy to Ojai.

BELLA MAGGIORE INN

67 S. California St.   Ventura, CA 93001   (805) 652-0277
Thomas J. Wood, Manager (800) 523-8479

LOCATION	Exit Hwy. 101 North at California St., right 1-1/2 blocks, or exit Hwy. 101 South at Ventura Ave., left to Thompson Blvd., left on California St.
OPEN	All Year
DESCRIPTION	1925 2-story Spanish Colonial Revival Mediterranean & Northern Italian furnishings
NO. OF ROOMS	25 w/private baths
RATES	$75-150 Reservation/cancellation policy
CREDIT CARDS	American Express, Diner's Club, MasterCard, Visa
BREAKFAST	Full, served in courtyard or dining/reception areas
AMENITIES	Sundeck roof garden; grand piano, fireplace & classical music in lobby; all rooms w/TV/radio, phones, ceiling fans & fresh flowers; some w/fireplace, wet bar, jacuzzi tubs, microwave, refrigerator & air conditioning; complimentary evening appetizers & beverages; conference/reception facilities; limited handicapped access
RESTRICTIONS	Smoking limited. No pets. Inquire about children
REVIEWED	*American Historic Bed & Breakfast Inns & Guesthouses* *America's Wonderful Little Hotels & Inns* *Bed & Breakfast in California* *Bed & Breakfast: Southern California* *Complete Guide to Bed & Breakfasts, Inns & Guesthouses*
RATED	AAA 3 Diamonds

LA MER EUROPEAN BED & BREAKFAST

411 Poli St.   Ventura CA, 93001
Gisela Flender Baida, Resident Owner

(805) 643-3600

LOCATION	On hillside facing intersection of Oak St., 3-1/2 blocks from beach
OPEN	All Year
DESCRIPTION	1890 2-story Cape Cod Victorian European antique furnishings
NO. OF ROOMS	5 w/private baths
RATES	Weekends/$80-155 Weekdays/$80-135 Reservation/cancellation policy Inquire about special mid-week packages & corporate rates
CREDIT CARDS	MasterCard, Visa
BREAKFAST	Full Bavarian, served in dining room, guestrooms, or on balconies & porches. Picnic baskets available
AMENITIES	European comforters, robes, radio in all rooms, fireplace in 1; complimentary wine; massage therapist & carriage rides available at extra charge
RESTRICTIONS	No smoking. No pets (resident outside dog, cat & bunnies). Children over 13
REVIEWED	*American Historic Bed & Breakfast Inns & Guesthouses* *America's Wonderful Little Hotels & Inns* *Bed & Breakfast in California* *Bed & Breakfast: Southern California* *Complete Guide to Bed & Breakfasts, Inns & Guesthouses* *Country Inns & Back Roads: California*
RATED	AAA 2 Diamonds Mobil 3 Stars

WEST COVINA
(LOS ANGELES)

This large community northeast of Los Angeles is a central access point into the San Gabriel Mountains Wilderness Area.

HENDRICK INN

2124 E. Merced Ave.   West Covina, CA 91791   (818) 919-2125
Mary & George Hendrick, Resident Owners

LOCATION	Exit I-10 at Azusa, north 2 mi. to Merced Ave., left (east) 2 blocks to home (map sent with confirmation)
OPEN	All Year
DESCRIPTION	1955 California Ranch Contemporary furnishings
NO. OF ROOMS	1 suite w/private bath 3 rooms share 2 baths
RATES	PB/$60 SB/$35-40 Reservation/cancellation policy 3-night minimum stay in suite
CREDIT CARDS	No
BREAKFAST	Full, served in kitchen, dining room, or on deck overlooking pool Dinner available w/advance notice
AMENITIES	Swimming pool, hot tub; fireplaces in common rooms; TV/radio in all rooms, phone in 2; complimentary refreshments; off-street parking
RESTRICTIONS	No smoking. No pets (resident dog). Children over 5
REVIEWED	*American Historic Bed & Breakfast Inns & Guesthouses* *Annual Directory of American Bed & Breakfast* *Bed & Breakfast Homes Directory: West Coast* *Bed & Breakfast in California* *Bed & Breakfast in the U.S.A. & Canada* *Bed & Breakfast U.S.A.* *Complete Guide to Bed & Breakfasts, Inns & Guesthouses*

WHITTIER
(LOS ANGELES)

One of the nicer small cities in the east central Los Angeles metroplex. Hop any freeway to get there.

COLEEN'S CALIFORNIA CASA

PO Box 9302   Whittier, CA 90608
Coleen Davis, Resident Owner
                                            (310) 699-8427

LOCATION	Exit 605 Freeway at Beverly East, east 10 blocks to Palm, left, then immediate right on Beverly Dr., 2 blocks to Rideout Way, left & up hill to South Circle Dr., left to home
OPEN	All Year
DESCRIPTION	1958 California split-level ranch Elegant furnishings
NO. OF ROOMS	3 w/private baths (including 1 suite)
RATES	$40-65 Reservation/cancellation policy 2-night minimum stay
CREDIT CARDS	No
BREAKFAST	Full, served in guestroom, on patio or deck
AMENITIES	Robes, TV/radio & phones in rooms; complimentary wine, cheese & soft drinks; meeting facilities; handicapped access
RESTRICTIONS	No smoking. No pets. Inquire about children
REVIEWED	*Bed & Breakfast Homes Directory: West Coast* *Bed & Breakfast in U.S.A. & Canada* *Bed & Breakfast: Southern California* *Bed & Breakfast U.S.A.* *Complete Guide to Bed & Breakfasts, Inns & Guesthouses* *Frommer's Bed & Breakfast: North America*
RSO	Co-Host: America's Bed & Breakfast
MEMBER	B&B Innkeepers of Southern California

WRIGHTWOOD

Escape the cityscapes into this nifty little town in the San Bernardino Mountains. The adjoining Big Pines Recreation Area offers all the good things of summer and skiing in the winter. From San Bernardino via I-15, Hwy. 138 and the designated scenic Angeles Crest Highway.

OGILVIE MANOR

1894 Ash Rd.   PO Box 475   Wrightwood, CA 92397   *(619) 249-6537*
Sheryl Ogilvie, Resident Owner

LOCATION	From Hwy. 138, 1 mi. west to Lone Pine Canyon Rd., 8 mi. to Heath Creek Rd., turn left & Manor is on the right
OPEN	All Year
DESCRIPTION	1989 2-story English Tudor English country furnishings
NO. OF ROOMS	2 w/private baths
RATES	$75 Reservation/cancellation policy 2-night minimum on weekends
CREDIT CARDS	No
BREAKFAST	Continental plus, served in dining room, gazebo or guestroom Afternoon tea available
AMENITIES	TV/radio in rooms
RESTRICTIONS	No smoking. No pets (resident cat). Inquire about children
REVIEWED	*Bed & Breakfast: Southern California*

ABOUT THE AUTHORS

TRAVIS ILSE was born near the headwaters of the Colorado River. He was neither caught in the 1968 Chicago police riot nor was he on the last chopper out of Saigon. He did not inhale. And while he is a conscientious letter writer, he does not return telephone calls, make appointments, or fly commercial airlines if he can help it. He lives in the Colorado mountains and looks down on Boulder.

TONI KNAPP was born in Bogota, Colombia and graduated from the University of San Francisco. She is the author of two children's books, *The Six Bridges of Humphrey the Whale* (Roberts Rinehart, Publishers), and *The Gossamer Tree*; and is the editor of *Absolutely Every° Bed & Breakfast in Arizona, Absolutely Every° Bed & Breakfast in California, Absolutely Every° Bed & Breakfast in Colorado, Absolutely Every° Bed & Breakfast in New Mexico* and *Absolutely Every° Bed & Breakfast in Texas (°Almost)*. She lives in Colorado Springs.

BED & BREAKFAST INDEX

ORDERING INFORMATION

If you would like additional copies of this book or other books in the series, please contact your local bookstore and give them all the information listed with each title. If the bookseller doesn't have the book in stock, she or he can get it for you in about a week to ten days.

THE ROCKY MOUNTAIN SERIES

Absolutely Every° Bed & Breakfast in Arizona (°Almost), Toni Knapp, editor, ISBN 1-882092-06-6, $12.95.

Absolutely Every° Bed & Breakfast in California, Monterey to San Diego (°Almost), Toni Knapp, editor, ISBN 1-882092-10-4, $15.95.

Absolutely Every° Bed & Breakfast in Colorado (°Almost), Toni Knapp, editor, ISBN 1-882092-08-2, $15.95.

Absolutely Every° Bed & Breakfast in New Mexico (°Almost), Toni Knapp, editor, ISBN 1-882092-07-4, $12.95.

Absolutely Every° Bed & Breakfast in Texas (°Almost), Toni Knapp, editor, ISBN 1-882092-09-0, $15.95.